Dear Jen,
Thank you for helping me find the perfect office space!

UNBOX

YOURSELF

Escape the Rat Race, Find More Happiness,
and Fulfill Your Purpose

You are awesome ☺

Christian Wolfram Hahn

J. Chris

Wolf Promedia

Prospect, Kentucky

Wolf Promedia
9527 U.S. Highway 42
Prospect, KY. 40059
info@freedomdoc.com

Book Layout ©2017 Book Design Templates
Copy editing by Stephanie Gunning
Cover design by Kostis Pavlou
Author photograph by Ben Marcum

Ordering Information:
Quantity sales. Special discounts are available on quantity purchases by corporations, associations, and others. For details, contact the "Special Sales Department" at the address above.

Unbox Yourself/ Christian W. Hahn. —1st ed.
ISBN 978-1-7320300-9-1 (paperback)

Library of Congress Control Number 2018903094

Contents

*To the souls that opened my eyes and
helped me unbox myself.*

You know who you are.

INTRODUCTION

"To live is the rarest thing in the world. Most people exist, that is all."

–Oscar Wilde

When I was in college, I didn't put much thought into choosing a career that would fulfill me. I took an aptitude test in high school that pointed me toward architecture, but I didn't pursue that career path. Instead I became a dentist. I then climbed the ladder of success only to realize that I felt trapped in my job. Something was missing. I wanted to molt my skin and start over. I wanted to discover the reason I was born and lead an epic life filled with adventure. To embody a purpose.

The exact reason I selected my profession is a blur to me. I don't have any memories of giving it deep thought or researching my options. To some extent, I suppose I was following in my father's footsteps. He was a dentist and provided well for our family, so I understood that dentistry offered a good income. From my observations of my dad's dental office, dentistry seemed great. Like him, I wanted to be my own boss. I got good grades and was accepted into the University of Southern California Dental School, my father's alma mater.

Fast forward twenty years to where I am today. Dentistry has been good to me and my wife and kids. Now in midlife, I have achieved success in my profession. I am at the pinnacle of my career. I lecture internationally about cosmetic dentistry. I run a successful, respected, fee-for-service dental practice where I am the boss. Every creature comfort you could want in life is at my disposal. So, theoretically, I could sail off into the sunset, practicing dentistry until retirement and die happy. End of story.

But that's not what my soul wants me to do. And it's not what a lot of other people in my situation are hungry for on a soul level either. There are those of us who long for the freedom to express ourselves and explore our potential in ways we perhaps have not done so since childhood. We long to escape the confines of our self-imposed limitations, take risks, and have adventures.

I have written this book for people, like me, who are awakening to a new sense of purpose. I have written it for people who are reevaluating their choices and contemplating trying something new: the pursuit of passion and meaning rather than stability and predictability; or in short, the pursuit of greatness.

On our deathbeds, none of us wants to look back on our lives with regret and say:

- "I wish I had the courage to live a life true to myself, not the life others expected of me."
- "I wish I hadn't worked so hard."
- "I wish I had the courage to express my feelings."
- "I wish I had stayed in touch with my friends."
- "I wish I had let myself be happier."

These are the top five regrets of dying patients, as reported by palliative care nurse Bronnie Ware in *The Top Five Regrets of the Dying*. Compare these regrets to the wish lists many of us have, which focus on achieving financial success. We hope to own a bigger house, a bigger car, more clothes, more jewelry, and have more prestige. What is the difference? If we look closely at the desires of the dying, a commonality is that the fulfillment of none requires money or social status. Working hard to gain material possessions is pointless in terms of happiness and satisfaction, whereas forming lasting friendships with people who accept us as we are and allow us to express ourselves authentically is priceless.

So why don't we all read these statements and immediately go out and make major changes in our lives? Especially if we feel that we're on the wrong path? I believe the reason we fail to act in ways that could generate more happiness for us is that we are deathly afraid of ego failure. We are more afraid of what others would *think of us* for altering our courses in life than we are of the possibility of failing in a new, more exhilarating venture. Peer pressure, real or perceived, is often so strong that we are willing to continue down the wrong path in our lives despite feeling miserable.

Taking the path of least resistance is another reason we remain boxed up in our lives. One decision flows from another until we find ourselves captured by comfortable restrictions of golden handcuffs. We don't want to risk losing what we already have. It is much easier and secure to stick with a job that pays the bill, even if it's not fulfilling, than to go out and start over from scratch in pursuit of your passion. It is much easier to stay on a well-worn path you're already familiar with than to beat a new path in virgin territory.

I was fortunate to learn early in my career that life is not about security, but about adventure, passion, joy, and love. When I was a new graduate, I landed a great position as the associate to one of the top dentists in Newport Beach, California. The man I worked for truly loved what he did and was a blessing to his patients. To this day, I am thankful to him and credit him for teaching me not only how to be a great dentist, but also, more importantly, how to communicate with people. He did not run the kind of "drill, fill, and bill" dental mill we see all over the place now. The ability to communicate with, and listen to, the people I serve as a dentist has been one of the main reasons why I am successful. It is the part of dentistry I enjoy the most. This, however, was not always the case. Initially, like most young professionals, I was excited to build my "empire" and become a successful, respected professional. Purpose and passion would have to wait a few years.

Back in the day, when the daughter of my employer got married, her reception was at the Ritz-Carlton Hotel. At the event, I found myself seated at a table with a veritable Who's Who of dentists of the day, speakers who got paid thousands by other dentists who wanted to learn from them. These were the dentists that every new graduate aspires to become like one day. And yet, that was the night that a seed was planted in my head—and heart—which kept growing for years, until it blossomed into the thought, *You don't want to end up like those guys.*

Why on earth would I not want to end up like those guys? They were rich, famous in the dental field, and by most measures had successful lives. Or did they?

The wedding was beautiful, fancy, and everything you'd expect at the Ritz. The wine was flowing freely, and it didn't take long for those at our table to drown their inhibitions. Seated in this circle, I was getting the inside scoop. And as I was listening to these big shots talk about their lives, it quickly became clear to me that dentistry had taken a significant toll on them. There was no talk about their favorite cases, the smiles they had rebuilt, the lives they had bettered, or their positive feelings. Instead, I distinctly remember them talking about their missed passions—hobbies they had formerly pursued and lost, like photography, and things they wanted to do but couldn't, like traveling, because they were handcuffed to their jobs by the need to maintain the lifestyles they had created around themselves. I recall hearing them talk about their first and second divorces, loneliness, and how much pain they felt from working as they did. Basically, they were miserable and felt stuck. One had survived a heart attack and was stressed to the max. Another quickly acknowledged feeling the same amount of stress.

Wow! I listened in disbelief, ultimately realizing there was no pot of gold at the end of the rainbow. I could see that my path of least resistance to the top of the dental field would lead me to a dead-end—and possibly off the edge of a cliff! The future these men were describing was a very scary proposition to me.

If it was true that the future I had hoped for throughout school was not the answer to happiness and fulfillment forever, then I would need to open my eyes and rethink certain aspects of my lifestyle.

That night changed my life because it set my mental wheels in motion. I moved slowly forward from that point, still pursuing the pinnacle of dentistry, however with a modicum of caution. Dentistry was my bread and butter, income wise, and yet I began exploring different passions and interests, such as inventing and problem solving. I did not know yet that these pathways would create new, more playful avenues of income for me one day. But they did enable me to explore my gifts.

Most people today would be shocked to hear that I was extremely shy as a teen. I am still an introvert, but talking to my patients every single day, all day long, for twenty years has brought me out of my shell. Furthermore, I find that I really enjoy helping people to conquer their limiting thought patterns and establish a healthier lifestyle. I am a trained cosmetic dentist and one of only 260 operating at my level of expertise. My passion has always been doing my own thing. I tell patients that I look at the holistic side of dentistry and the scientific side of things and straddle the gap between.

Tooth wise, I've always been guiding my patients. But more and more people come to me for personal consultations on healing their bodies and minds. We speak about their lives and how they can reduce stress. I explain how the stress they feel is affecting their mouths by producing acidity and leading them to grind their teeth—and what they can do to heal. If they've been going on autopilot for a while before awakening to the fact that they're not happy, making lifestyle changes is essential.

Some people compensate for boredom and unhappiness at midlife by signing up for dance lessons, buying a fast car, and traveling more. Most don't pick up one day and move to the jungle of Bolivia. Some version of their lives continues. But what they really would like to know is, "How can I get out of this rut and create something new without ruining my whole life?"

It took me until recently to understand why my professional satisfaction is above average. By then, I had almost reached the same level in my career as those dentists with whom I had sat at the wedding of my boss's daughter. Because of exploring my creative gifts and expressing myself authentically, playfully, and passionately throughout my career, I had avoided getting caught up in the traps that many in my profession fall into by midlife or midway into their careers as dentists.

There is an astonishing rate of suicide among dentists. At its worst, after a few years the procedures become routine. As a dentist, you work in a small room, possibly windowless, that's analogous to a jail cell. You're bent forward over people's mouths the whole time you're working, so your shoulders hurt, your arms hurt, and your eyes hurt. And you start going deaf due to the sounds of the instruments after a while. The routine is the same every day.

Also, most of the people you see really do not want to see you. They may tell you, "It's nothing personal, but I hate coming in." Or they're anxious and afraid of you. They don't do as you advise; none floss or brush as they're supposed to—and neither do you, probably. You may also feel very isolated because you're the boss and everybody in your office works for you—so they're not your friends or peers. You have no one with whom to shoot the breeze.

Connection doesn't happen through networking either. Local dentists don't communicate well with one another because they're in competition for clients. As their bodies slowly fail, their enthusiasm for the art of dentistry wanes and their skills deteriorate. Meanwhile, chances are good that they are living a lifestyle that's exactly at or above their means, spending at least as much, and possibly more, than they make. Thus, they worry about the future. They may want to cut back on their workloads, yet they do not feel that they can.

Just a few decades ago, dentists and doctors were making the most money of anyone. Today, it's app developers and social network builders. Of all types of health professionals, dentists tend to work the longest hours because they don't scale their businesses correctly. And it's hard to get out of this pattern. Their kids go to private schools and they've taken membership in a country club. They've got house and car payments to make. It's the golden-handcuff paradigm, a vicious cycle of trying to make enough to pay for your obligations.

The good news is that there is a way to release the cuffs and unbox yourself. This way has to do with self-examination and waking up to the potential inherent to your life.

Unboxing Yourself is the first book in a three-book series designed to mirror the stages of life we all traverse once we've realized that something is not right: Explore, Challenge, and Transcend. At some point, we decide that life should have more meaning, be more fulfilling, and be less stressful. We ask, *What is the purpose of my life?*

This moment can happen early on or as we take our last breath. Whenever it arrives, we have a choice to make: Do we harness the power of the most powerful word in any language—*why*—and begin asking questions and exploring who we really are, why we were born, and what our purpose is? Or do we let the awakening pass and go with the flow, following the herd—possibly over the edge of the next cliff?

Exploring who you are is what unboxing yourself is all about. This is the quest of finding yourself, discovering your gifts, and identifying your purpose.

Having identified who you really are and what you want out of life is just the beginning. Subsequent action is then required for you to achieve your goals and arrive at your destination. You will have to challenge yourself, to push yourself to act so that you can learn and grow.

When we start to see life as a series of situations consisting of choices rather than good or bad problems, then you will know you have entered the final stage of your maturation. At this point, you will focus on acceptance, forgiveness, and love. Your ego will be reduced to a faint whisper in the back of your mind and it will no longer have the deciding vote in your daily activities. You will see the world as it really is, as a sequence of amazing events designed by you yourself to grow your consciousness. This is the stage when you will transcend into your full potential. You will be living as your true self.

Transcendence does not mean becoming a monk. It means moving from a life in a box, restricted and controlled by your ego, to being at peace with your existence regardless of your circumstances and allowing your consciousness to guide you completely.

This book is designed to walk you through the first steps of exploration of who you really are: an amazing spiritual being.

1 PLAN A VS. PLAN B

"Imagination is more important than knowledge."

−**Albert Einstein**

Life is an adventure . . . or so it should be. For too many of us it's not. Most of us undergo a critical change sometime in our teenage years. That's when we are asked to *relinquish our dreams* and begin planning a *realistic life.*

At six, kids love *Star Wars,* believes in Santa Claus, and go from wanting to become president of the United States to inventing a flying car, on a whim. Their imagination is on overdrive. These young minds are on the right track to invent the next light bulb, airplane, or Tesla coil! Then the change begins . . . adults begin telling the child, "That is some imagination you have there. Why don't you try to be more *realistic* about *your* future? Have you thought about being a doctor? A lawyer? Maybe an accountant?"

The constant belittling and criticizing of the imagination by adults who don't have much of one themselves anymore usually manages to shift children toward the *realistic* life plan that those adults feel would result in a stable, successful life.

Let me try to sell you on this stable life plan, Plan A, and see if you would buy it now, knowing what you know with your current life experience. There is a Plan B, but it is not offered to many children by adults.

Plan A: The Stable Life Plan

With Plan A, you are allowed a normal childhood with unrestricted dreams until about age eleven. At this point you are expected to begin "growing up." You take the same classes as every other child. You are tested and compared to your peers. The results of standardized testing will have a significant impact on your ability to get more education, which hopefully leads to a better/higher paying job.

In high school, you get some career counseling. You are exposed to a wide selection of careers, most of which require you to work for someone else (likely someone that picked Plan B, which we'll get to shortly). You may go on to college, a trade school, a graduate school. In the Plan A job, you will work forty hours or more per week, beginning immediately after completing your education. Often the more your job pays, the more hours you will be expected to work by your employer.

You will receive an average of one to two weeks of paid vacation per year, and five days off for federal holidays. You will perform this job for several decades, the bulk of your life, probably not stopping until about age seventy, at which point you will retire. The government will have taken a small portion of your income throughout your life, and this will now slowly be returned to you to help you live the rest of your life far below the level to which you have become accustomed.

The average American male lifespan is seventy-nine years, which gives you about nine years to live after retirement. Most of those years will probably be taken up with doctor visits and low mobility, but heck, they are your golden years. Live it up, you earned the rest!

Now, having read my description of Plan A, are you sold? Perhaps this plan sounds something like the career path you're currently on. If so, how is that working out for you?

Before you buy, let's take a similar look at the alternate career plan.

Plan B: Personalized/ Purpose Driven Life Plan

With Plan B, as with Plan A, you are allowed a childhood with unrestricted dreams. There will never be any restrictions on your dreams. And in fact, your dreams will be nurtured and encouraged forever. Your parents and teachers focus on helping you discover your gifts and talents, and then on showing you how to build your life around a self-defined purpose. Testing in school is tailored toward understanding your strengths. You are rarely expected to undergo standardized testing (only when the state or federal law requires it) because it's obvious to your caregivers that one cannot compare the ability of a cat and a fish to climb a tree. You are treated as the unique individual you are.

In high school, you get some career counseling. You may also be introduced to mentors who give you internships and be taught business skills. You are exposed to diverse people and the arts. Your parents tell you that you can be and do anything you want. You also may be encouraged to take time off from school to travel and explore the world.

Once you have selected a path through life that maximizes your gift and fills you with purpose and excitement—including the path of going to school to get appropriate training and degrees before or during the stage at which initial moneymaking begins—you embark on changing the world at your pace. You may work three days a week or seven days a week on the projects that utilize and amplify your primary skills and interests, depending on your resources. You'll work on your endeavors in your spare time, if you must, to get them up and running. The time and energy you expend won't matter to you so long as you are pursuing your passion and purpose, not just money.

As a matter of fact, the work you will do really should not be called *work*. It should be called *living*. Most likely you will dance to your own tune and won't have a boss. Many, if not most highly successful entrepreneurs, people such as Richard Branson, Mark Zuckerberg, J.K. Rowling, and Sarah Kauss, chose this path. You may retire at thirty or you may never retire at all; this is up to you. You may start more than one business. Some will fail. Some will succeed.

Like people on Plan A, after a certain age—somewhere around sixty-five or seventy—you will begin to receive periodic installments that return the small amount of money the government took from you during your career. But you most likely will not need these funds, as you have built a successful career and planned for this stage of your life.

Life will not be about waiting to retire and live a few years in your seventies going to doctors and complaining about your health or spending your wealth to regain the health you spent building your wealth. Rather, it will be about living every day as if it was your last on earth and never even using the word *retirement* because you love what you do.

If you're feeling boxed in and stuck right now, I bet that Plan B seems more appealing than Plan A to you based on comparing these descriptions. It sure does to me. Most of the spice in life—adventure, invention, exploration, and imagination—comes from pursuing Plan B.

Which plan are you buying?

Which Plan Are You On?

Most people are pushed into Plan A and never are given—or take—the opportunity to consider Plan B. Are you one of them? I invite you to consider Plan B now. Which plan are you on? Are you happy?

If not, there's good news. You can switch plans anytime!

Bottom line, this book is for individuals who want to switch from Plan A to Plan B and are looking for a roadmap. If you are that person—stuck in Plan A and wanting to make a change—this moment here is your fork in the road. You've got to choose it. Once you have the awareness that Plan B is possible, a whole bunch of options become available to you. There are no coincidences in life and the fact that you are reading this book alone is a step into the right direction.

Do you remember the scene in *The Matrix,* where Morpheus (played by Laurence Fishburne) offers Neo (played by Keanu Reeves) the choice of a red pill or a blue pill? He says words to the effect of, "Do you want to take the red pill and find out what really is going on or do you want to take the blue pill and wake up inside the Matrix with no memory that there was a greater reality outside it?" Well, I am offering you a similar choice in this moment.

The Matrix in the film is a giant computer run by using human bodies and brains for its batteries, and the people think they are living in our world, which is just a computer simulation! Like them, Plan A people live in a simulation, or a box, which limits their ability to blossom into their full potential and experience true freedom. To change to Plan B, to "take the red pill," you need first to *become aware* of the fact that you are stuck in a false reality and muster up the desire to break free.

Think of me as your personal Morpheus, asking you the important question.

Do you want to wake up to everything that is possible, follow the path of Plan B—where you can find out what life really is about—or would you rather "take the blue pill," stay in your box, go back to Plan A, where you can live a straightforward, relatively unambitious life and go on simply existing day after day, year after year?

Obviously, I am encouraging you to "take the red pill" and embark on the adventure that your life was meant to be. Do it!

There truly is a qualitative difference between existing and living. And if you need proof, simply look around you. Everything you can see and touch was created by someone on Plan B who felt the need to make a difference—every invention, product, business, song . . . everything you love, everything you hate. Everything.

What Happens Next?

After you take the red pill and become aware that Plan B is a real option (because many happy and successful people live this plan), you will need to build your skills, explore your options, and seek guidance from appropriate individuals so that you constantly move in the direction of your dreams and goals. This book is all *"red pill,"* so you are already on the right track!

Plan B will be an exciting journey for you. But be forewarned, once you leave the Matrix things are going to change. Some of your friends, family, and acquaintances on Plan A will resent you switching to Plan B. Maybe from envy, maybe from fear of being abandoned, they could try to change your mind by belittling your choices and objectives.

Why would they do this? Mainly because they feel the need to be right. If someone is succeeding and we are not (from our own perspective), then resentment and jealousy can take over. It's the way the human mind (the ego part) works. We feel best when we are surrounded by likeminded individuals whose presence reinforces the idea that what we are doing is right.

In a Plan B life, there are times when we want to give up. It's normal. During critical times, it is important to reach out to someone that is on Plan B like you and ask them to support you and encourage you in your venture. Surround yourself with happy, likeminded individuals and this journey will be amazing. Dump the critics. Remember, most people go through life *existing,* whereas *living* life is one of the rarest experiences of all.

2 STARTING OVER

"Freedom's just another word for nothing left to lose."

–**Fred Foster and Kris Kristofferson**

Something happens to most people usually in our early forties. We question our paths and begin wanting to do many of the things we did and enjoyed when we were younger. We look at our careers and our personal choices and we wonder, *Am I doing what I am supposed to do? Am I doing the things that will make me happy?* We sense the passage of time and do not want to waste a precious minute. The fear of living a meaningless life of regret no longer can be ignored.

Friends and colleagues that live in the same boxes that we do—including our spouses—may try to reassure us that the rat race we're all running together is fine or that we are just going through a phase and in a while everything will go back to normal. Those close to us may feel frightened by the changes they see in our patterns of behavior and the new interests we start developing, because they are counting on us to be predictable. Some view our critical course corrections as crises. But let's call this phenomenon what it really is: a *midlife awakening*.

What is a midlife awakening? It's a last-ditch effort by the soul to inspire us to live the exciting and passionate lives we dreamed of as children and came to this earth for, as opposed to the predictable, boring, stressful lives most people would call normal.

There is nothing normal, great, or honorable about living a life that is not fulfilling. Nothing.

But how will you know when you are ready to press the RESET button in your life? If you're like most people at midlife, for years, if not decades, your life may have been so busy that you never had the chance to pause and really think about where you were heading. At some point, you may have begun to realize that something was missing. You may have noticed that your bucket list is still quite long, and time is running out. Eventually, hopefully, you also realized that you needed to do something different before it was too late.

I hit the mark of wanting to unbox myself a few times before making any changes in my life because the fear of change—which is no joke—beat me back into submission and forced me to stick with what I knew. Switching to a purpose-driven life was not as easy for me as some people have made it sound.

Many people want and need to make drastic changes in their lifestyles, but they still think they can redecorate the box they live inside instead of unboxing themselves. True freedom forces us to build lives around our soul's purpose, which means we must be willing to let everything go and follow our intuition. In some cases, this requires us to make drastic changes.

"Achieve financial independence."

"Work when and where you want."

"Love your job."

"Live a life of meaning."

These slogans clearly are goals for most of us, including myself, but unfortunately are often used in advertising to draw us into the newest get-rich quick scheme, which in truth likely is designed to make someone else rich instead of us. They work on us because they express our innermost desires. But I should warn you, if you start your journey of awakening by focusing primarily on money, rather than on purpose, then you likely will fail to unbox yourself, even if you make a lot of money.

How do you avoid this trap and still reap the promised rewards that we all seek? Unbox yourself first, find out what drives you, and then fuel your desire with purpose and action. This may be as simple as restructuring how you do what you do or as complex as making a career change.

Do not settle for a box; instead, aim for the freedom of self-expression. Unboxing yourself leads to a more purpose-driven life, a life defined by simply being who we were born to be—no more and no less.

The lure of money, especially when we need it, is often too much to resist. We need money to cover our house payments, the tuition for our kids' schools, vacations, cars, and clothes, even Starbucks coffee. The burden of keeping up with a certain quality of life that we were taught and came to believe mattered weighs on us until we feel money is the only answer. And sure, money will alleviate these financial pressures, at least temporarily.

But at some point, if we are to escape the pressure entirely, we need to make the shift away from a materialistic lifestyle, where we define ourselves egocentrically through what we own and can spend, and move toward leading a more fulfilling, consciously lived life.

Being conscious does not automatically mean that one has less money to spend—although it could mean that. It means that your fulfillment and your money is sourced from using your natural gifts and creativity rather than from obediently doing what was expected of you when you were a kid. Money is treated as a tool, not an obsession.

It only gets more difficult with time to let go of the status we build for ourselves professionally. Is it easy to admit that you don't value the things you've been doing since you started your career? Heck no! It might be one of the most difficult, uncomfortable experiences of your life to give up a profession that brought you admiration and gave structure to your days. To shift from a Plan A to a Plan B lifestyle, you may need to break through so many of your comfort barriers that at some point you could run down Hollywood Boulevard naked and feel more comfortable.

But when you emerge from your box at the end of the journey of exploring your values, *you will be living as your true self rather than a reflection of other people's expectations.* This is a more comfortable way to live because it requires much less effort.

Finding your personal gifts does not have to be complicated. You have many gifts, so you cannot go wrong. Just think about what you are good at and what you enjoy doing. What lights your fire? When you wake up on a beautiful day, what can't you wait to do? The gift that would give you a strong sense of purpose simply is something you do very well that makes you happy as well as everyone you share it with. It could be cooking, speaking, a sport, a profession, or just about anything else.

When you sink your energy into your gift, amazing things will happen.

There, of course, will be challenges and roadblocks throughout the journey to unbox yourself. While sharing your gift with the world may bring you happiness, it could also pad your ego. This can open an entirely new can of worms. Our society is aware of the ego. It is impossible for us to escape the constant play to get its attention. Everywhere we turn, someone is trying to sell us something by stroking our egos. I wonder how many of the kind of get-rich-quick schemes that the ego loves result in happy lives? Even if we begin to taste success, it is a double-edged sword that makes ego management very difficult.

When we embark on our individual journeys to lead lives worth living, we encounter many challenges, the ego being one of the more significant ones we must overcome.

Fortunately, the journey is the essence of life, not the destination. Each challenge we encounter is crafted to give us an opportunity to make the decision to drop the influence of the ego and follow the soul's desires. Detours are fine, and even fun, but we should make a course correction as soon as possible and always do our best to keep the goal of improving the quality of our consciousness in mind.

One of the biggest challenges I faced when I first caught on to the purpose of my life was not identifying the parameters of my box but figuring out how to incorporate my *freedom business*—by definition, a business or career that you cannot wait to attend to each day because it is your passion—into my already busy life. There are few things scarier than deciding to make a career change when you have three children in private school and need a high-income job to fund their education. I worried: *How will I support my family? Is it even possible to start over and maintain a similar quality of life?*

This has got to be the most common worry for those of us who are about to change course: How do we make the transition without losing everything we have and failing to meet our responsibilities? How will we make the money required? The solution for it is to change how we look at our goals. We do not need to drop everything and start over immediately, just to focus on unboxing ourselves and making daily progress, while accepting the current situation "as is" and being thankful/grateful for what we have.

Begin surrounding yourself by individuals who already make a good living doing what you are considering and allow them to have such a positive impact on you that you cannot help following in their footsteps.

It is always necessary to change our mindset—our thoughts and emotions—first. We do not need to have all the answers to get started. All we need is a clear understanding of where we want to be in the future. Not a wish. Not a hope. A clear understanding. We need to get excited for what will happen and then to act emotionally as if it already has.

We are the architects of everything in our lives. The mind leads, and the body follows.

My transition began with a swimming lesson. My daughter was about six years old at the time, and I was sitting at the edge of a cloudy baby pool, waiting for her learn-to-swim lesson to begin. All the parents were sitting with their children and fussing with their hair, their suits, and their swim goggles, while at the same time trying to tell them the class would be fun. The room was hot and humid, and you could have cut the tension with a knife. I myself was struggling with a pair of flimsy swim goggles, trying to fit them onto my daughter's head without ripping out her hair, which turned out to be impossible. The rubber straps pulled her hair in such a way that adjusting them was impossible. I was getting more stressed by the minute, and as I looked around the room I realized that everybody else was having the same issue.

This theoretically amazing experience of my daughter learning how to swim was anything but magical because of those goggles. In fact, it was a stress fest and certainly not worth capturing on film—no Facebook or Instagram filter could have made the scene pretty.

After the lesson, I went home and told myself there had to be a better way. The goggle dilemma was way too stressful for anyone to be able to enjoy the experience of swimming. Then it came to me: I would invent comfortable swim goggles! It had to be possible. I went downstairs into the basement and pulled out some of my old wetsuits, which had travelled with me from California to Kentucky and now were sitting in a box down there idle. I cut them up and began sewing together different neoprene strap designs aiming to find one that would gently glide over hair without pulling on it.

After several hours of cutting, sewing, and gluing, I had designed a crude prototype that I was eager to try out on my children's heads. It worked. The straps were perfect, and their hair didn't pull.

For the next few months, I worked daily on my design, until I had both a comfortable and a cool-looking design. My kids were the test subjects and got to wear the different designs to the pool for those months. What troopers they were!

The design was so good that I received a utility patent for it in 2013 and built a company around it, Made By My Dad LLC. I called the new swim goggles Frogglez and they quickly became a bestseller in the market. As it turns out, the problem I had identified was a problem most parents had, not just me and the parents in my daughter's swim class.

One of my gifts in life is that I am inventive. I love solving problems and creating things that make life better. As soon as I pursued this passion, my invention took off and my new company gave me the ability to unbox myself from being identified exclusively as a cosmetic dentist. Without Made By My Dad, it would have been significantly more difficult for me to make a life change.

Once I had the company up and running out of the back of my dental office between patients, I had to decide, *Do I completely focus on this new company or keep splitting my time between both ventures?* Running two companies at the same time, each demanding 100 percent of my focus, was initially very stressful. Not until I did some soul searching did I realize I now had the opportunity to unbox myself and be free. For me, freedom includes financial independence and living a purpose-driven life—no debt, no loans, just living in the now and fearlessly exploring all that life offers.

Looking back on my decision, I realize that everything changed once I acted. Manufacturing and selling Frogglez goggles to stores and consumers was not always easy, but I kept moving forward with the project until it became a success. Regarding splitting my focus in half and trying to do everything for two businesses simultaneously, well, I found a solution that works for my life: I built a team of people who shared my core values and work ethic. I began hiring people smarter than me at what they did and stopped trying to micromanage everything.

Focusing on my personal strengths and delegating everything else to the team changed my world. I wanted a business that I could run virtually from the beach, a coffee shop, or while traveling the world—and I was fine if my team wanted to work in the same ways. You would be surprised how many people wanted to be part of a business like this.

Now, I must admit that Frogglez was not my first invention. Invention has been part of my daily existence for several decades. I feel as if I cannot help but reinvent everything I see and touch. This can be quite annoying to me and those closest to me on occasion. I have journals filled with hundreds of documented inventions and solutions to the problems I encounter daily. Once an idea enters my mind, I need to get it down on paper, so it can leave my mind. Otherwise I obsess about it for weeks.

The reason Frogglez became successful has nothing to do with it being one of the better ideas I've had and everything to do with the fact that my wife told me to quit dabbling with hundreds of other ideas and focus on this one. Thanks, honey!

Sinking my teeth into making Frogglez goggles is what brought the idea and company to life. Nothing would have happened if I had not had someone to guide me and point me into the right direction, so I am extremely thankful for my wife's vision and support. At some point, we all could use some help and a gentle push to focus and take action!

Discovering our talents and gifts and putting all our weight behind them enables us to move mountains. Support from other people, like my team and my wife, sustains us so we can go the distance.

Your hobby has the potential to turn into a career if you want it to be one. It does not matter if your passion is a love for cars or gourmet cooking. Someone somewhere has done what you want to do before you. Therefore, it is possible. The secret ingredient is simply to get started and then take daily action.

Your midlife awakening is a gift that may scare the conformists you know to death! But don't worry about them. Later, you won't regret the risks you took but the risks you did not take. Pursue your opportunities with all the might you can muster, as this is how to unbox yourself.

3 IDENTIFYING YOUR BOX

"You'll never know who you are unless you shed who you pretend to be."
–Vironika Tugaleva

Most people are capable of reading a roadmap. To use a map to get somewhere, all you must do is find out where you currently are on the map (point A) and where you want to go (point B), and then pick a path between them. Simple, right?

And travel is simpler still when you have a GPS-enabled app on your smartphone that tells you what to do: "Turn right. Turn left. Go straight ahead for twenty feet."

Now, let's look at life. It doesn't come with a map—at least not a good one. We all have lots of dreams, goals, and aspirations. Some of us want to make money, become famous, or find the perfect match. Some of us want to help people. Some of us just want to be happy without striving much. Your goals in life can be anything; it really does not matter. You may think about your goal every day, wishing you could find your way, a secret formula. But wishing isn't a plan. Most of us just flounder around, trying this and that, without really making much progress toward our goals because we are lacking a crucial tool: a "map." Without the information it provides, our steps are random.

Imagine this. If someone asked you, could you navigate to New York City using only a roadmap? Your answer would be, yes, of course.

Great, let's give it a shot. We will blindfold you, plop you down in the middle of a desert out West, hand you the roadmap, and ask you to pick your route to the East Coast. What will you do now?

Most likely you'll ask, "Where am I?" This is a natural first question. You want to find point A on your map. Why do we need this critical piece of information? Because without it, your roadmap will be useless.

Life is a bit more complex than this, but the analogy still works. We simply have no chance of arriving at a desired destination unless we know exactly where we are coming from. The destination and the starting point lead us to the path.

If you want to become a doctor, you can't simply take the national boards and get certified as a physician. You also must complete other, necessary steps that are part of the medical school curriculum.

If you are in high school in the United States, your path will be different from someone who lives in another country and has already earned a doctoral degree. Even if two people want to end up in the same career, doing similar jobs, if they have very different starting points, they may have to find different ways to reach the same destination.

Not identifying the starting point, the destination, and the path only results in failure and frustration. Sometimes we get motivated by the successes of people who found their paths and already are arriving at their destinations. They are making the amount of money we want to make or living aspects of the lifestyles we desire, so we hone in on the specific route they took to get where they are, thinking, *If they can do it, so can I.* We set out to duplicate their success by following their roadmap. But what happens? Failure, most likely. Why? Because we are starting from a different place than them.

Your path through life is unique and will be different than anyone else's path. Everybody has different talents, passions, skills, and resources that define their starting points. When we try to follow a path that doesn't belong to us, we are, in fact, putting ourselves in a new box rather than liberating ourselves to find fulfillment through the freedom of a spontaneous, meaningful path. That's just nuts. Crazy.

What Is a Box?

Your first step in this chapter is to identify your starting point, who you currently are and why. What you stand for, what role you play in society and how you are perceived by others. This is what we are coining your *current box.*

What is a box? Our box could also be described as a mask. The box we live in and the mask we wear are essentially the same thing. Both are self-generated, and therefore, only skin deep. The mask is the image we portray to others to please them. It is carefully sculpted by the ego, which often does not account for what we ourselves truly want because we are so afraid of the prospect of triggering other people's critical judgment of us. We work hard at building our boxes and putting on masks that suit other people's opinions. Sadly, we end up smothering our souls. The best of us become good at putting on amazing shows.

Our attempts to match the expectations of the society we live in –our outer reality—do not necessarily represent who we are at our core—our inner reality. For some of us, the outer and inner realities are closer than for others, but everyone tries to fit in to some degree to be successful.

What if I told you the mask you are wearing is really a mirror?

Imagine you are looking at a mirrored box. Each side of this box reflects everything around it perfectly. Inside the box lives the soul of a person, which is well-hidden from onlookers, like you, because all they see when they look at it is an image of their own beliefs, hopes, and dreams. The reflection of themselves emanating from the walls of the box is so mesmerizing that most people never even know the soul inside the box is there. And the soul living in the box is relieved. It feels safe in its disguise, albeit restricted in its expression.

In general, people see what they want when they look at us or interact with us. We do not let them see the inner reality we have hidden unless we unbox ourselves.

Ever since childhood, we have been building our mirrored boxes based on outside influences. Layer after layer, we carefully craft these boxes to match the expectations of the people in our lives. These expectations continually get ingrained in us. Each opinion, comment, and suggestion has been noted by us and incorporated. For example, if our parents say something like, "You are tall and would make a great basketball player," we take note of this, using it to identify how "tall" people should be. If we're living in a box, we may attach the label of "basketball player" to ourselves and then behave like we think a basketball player should behave—even if personally we feel more attracted to playing soccer or doing yoga.

Each layer of the box built from external influences like these affects our thinking and decisions, gradually pushing us to match the image in our minds of who we should be. The more closely we match the image, the more deeply we bury our authentic selves. This limits us from becoming what we would naturally become if we were living spontaneously.

Every child is born with certain gifts that are not easily discernable at first. Imagine a nursery in which three newly born babies are lying next to each other. While they may look similar, their gifts are vastly different. One is destined to become a NBA star, another to cure cancer, and so forth. They each have unique talents that they need to discover and hopefully use to lead a life of greatness. Pushing the natural athlete towards becoming a math wizard is not be the best course of action unless he also has a gift for numbers.

Everybody is a genius. If you judge a fish by its ability to climb a tree, it will live its whole life believing that it is stupid.

Letting children discover if they are fishes, birds, or tigers is essential for their success and happiness in this world. When our gifts emerge from within, the mirrored boxes we live inside look closer to the truth of who we are. And even though you are an adult now, you can connect with the inner fish, bird, or tiger in you—metaphorically speaking—and let it out of the box.

In *Skillful Means*, Tibetan Buddhist teacher Tarthang Tulku summarizes the social process. "Our obstacles to inner freedom are usually formed during childhood. As children we know how we feel about things, and we seldom hesitate to make our feelings known. But pressure from family and friends leads us to adopt the more narrow views and patterns that conform to what people expect. When our *natural ideas and feelings* are discouraged, we grow out of touch with our senses, and the flow of communication between our bodies and minds is inhibited; we no longer know what we truly feel. As the patterns of suppression grow stronger and more *fixed,* our opportunities for self-expression diminish. We become so used to conforming, that as we grow older we let these patterns rule our lives; we become strangers to ourselves."[1]

In some instances, we can deceive ourselves into thinking we are leading authentic lives because we have built our box from the desires of our egos. For instance, I asked a friend of mine how he picked his path towards success and he said, "When I was a child I went up to expensive cars and asked the drivers what they did for a living." Whatever that driver described was the box that he then jumped into. This anecdote reminds me of the Jim Carrey quote "I think everybody should get rich and famous and do everything they ever dreamed of so they can see that it's not the answer."[2]

At some point, our boxes have become solid reflections of the labels placed upon us by the people we socialize with and emulate. And after years of building boxes that have hidden our true selves deeply, we have forgotten who we really are. We proudly wear these boxes like suits of armor to defend ourselves from the uncertainty of life. And this is how we define ourselves.

To define ourselves in terms of a career, we use easy-to-understand terms like *accountant* or *doctor*. To define ourselves in terms of a personality, we use terms like *shy* or *outgoing*. The idea being that everyone we know is in general agreement with what those words mean.

But how did we arrive at such well-defined definitions of ourselves? From following the path of least resistance. We wanted to fit in, to please our friends and family. And later to impress our teachers and employers, and our peers.

How can you find out what your box is? In two ways. First, by analyzing what you know about your activities. Second, by asking the people in your life for help to describe you. What you believe your box is and what everyone else sees and experiences may be completely different.

Evaluating Your Box for Yourself

Now, prior to asking your peers who you are, ask yourself some questions. The point is to find out what you stand for. Answer these questions for how your life currently is—not for last year or how you want your life to be in the future. Write down your responses. It is important to get as accurate a starting point for your journey to unbox yourself as possible.

Answering some of these questions may require you to do a little research. Just be as accurate as you can.

Ask:

- How much money do I make?
- How much time off/vacation do I get?
- How many hours per week do I work?
- What hobbies do I actively engage in?
- Do I eat healthily?
- Do I exercise?
- Do I meditate?
- Do I have a morning routine? What is it?
- Do I continue to educate myself through books, podcasts, and videos?

- Do I still dream? What do I dream of?
- What are three items in my "bucket list" (must-dos before dying)?
- Where do I see myself in three months, six months, and one year (in terms of my finances, work, relationships, and happiness)?

Asking Your Community to Help You Recognize Your Box

Now, it's time to ask the people that helped you build your box what they think you stand for. You can ask your friends, your colleagues at work, and your family members some basic questions that will quickly reveal the person they think you are.

Yes, they probably will wonder why you are asking such stupid questions (since you already know most of the answers), so make a game out of it. People love games and competition. The only rule is that everyone needs to be completely honest. No sugar coating the truth to avoid upsetting you or brown nosing you to puff up your ego is allowed. Making the answers anonymous through a blind survey is a great way to get honest answers.

Ask:

- How much money do I make?
- How much time off/vacation do I get?
- How many hours per week do I work?
- What hobbies do I actively engage in?

- Do I eat healthily?
- Do I exercise?
- Do I meditate?
- Do I have a morning routine? What is it?
- Do I continue to educate myself through books, podcasts, and videos?
- Do I still dream? What do I dream of?
- What are three items in my "bucket list" (must-dos before dying)?
- Where do I see myself in three months, six months, and one year? (In terms of my finances, work, relationships, and happiness)

Ask the same, simple, leading questions and be open to receiving honest answers. Feel free to ask as many questions as you like of each person—or as few. Ask additional questions as they come to mind. Remain calm and respectful and listen to the answers if you are face to face. Or send out an anonymous survey.

We are often surprised to learn what others think about us. Consider it your good fortune if you learn something new during this process.

Now we have two perspectives of self—how we see ourselves and what the outside world sees: our reflection. If you have low self-esteem, as seen in depression and other illnesses, realize that finding out who you are inside, below this layer of self-doubt, is how you can build self-love and find yourself. It is ideal if the world can see our true inner selves, but the need to fit in and reflect an image that will please those around us is strong and hard to resist Asking these questions of ourselves before we ask those who spend time around us helps us gauge how different our inner and outer personas are, which consequentially gives us a starting point and ending point in the journey to explore and then express our true inner selves.

Being unboxed is something you can really look forward to because this way of living will be so much more aligned with what makes you happy. You will know you are unboxed when you don't care what other people think and stop accommodating the people all around you who want something from you.

A story I once heard helped me initially understand the concept of the mirrored box. It is a story about an eagle that was born among a brood of chickens. As a baby, he looked like all the other chicks around him, but as he grew up he began to look and feel different. He had stronger wings, talons instead of claws, and a nagging desire to soar the skies. Yet because of growing up around brothers and sisters who were content to peck at the ground for their sustenance, he suppressed his desire and mimicked what they were doing.

The teenage chickens made fun of the teenage eagle's appearance and behavior regardless of how hard he tried to fit in. Being ridiculed and teased made him feel so poorly about himself that he redoubled his efforts to prove that he was a good chicken "just like you," clucking and picking at the dirt as well as he could.

One day the young eagle saw another eagle soar above the brood and he asked his chicken siblings what kind of bird it was. The chickens told him that was an eagle and that they were only chickens and could not fly like that. They told him: *Neither could he.*

This is the turning point of the story, a moment when the eagle could decide that he wanted to live in disguise as a chicken or as the eagle he knew deep down that he was. What he did next depended on how much he wanted to stay with his brood. The choice was entirely his: Unbox himself (remove the mask, stop being complacent and people-pleasing, and step out of the mirrored box) or continue living a life in which he was not being true to himself.

If you are on the journey to explore your true nature, you are this eagle, and you get to decide if you want to soar or not—however "soaring" looks when you express your own gifts.

If your true inner self is being expressed completely—meaning, people can see you exactly as you see yourself—then effectively, you do not live inside a box. This is freedom.

When we compare who we are at the core, our "eagle" selves, to who we have become from trying to be "good chickens," these identities may be very different or very similar. The bigger the difference there is between expressing our natural gifts and desires doing things that are acceptable to our family members and communities, the more walls we will have to break through if we want to unbox ourselves and explore our natural potential. The walls we build around us to disguise our true selves from the people we know and want to please keep us from pursuing our true dreams and passions. They are obstacles to taking the journey of expressing our true selves.

After tearing down the walls that we hide behind, life becomes easier and just seems to flow. We behave naturally, have more energy, and make decisions spontaneously.

Use the information you obtained while doing your exercise to create a chart. On one side, put your starting point, which is the reflection of you, as you are living today, described by your family, friends, and colleagues.

Put your one-year goals on the other side of the page. Even if these do not yet reflect your core self—who you believe and feel inside that you were born to be—they will demonstrate to you what you currently believe is possible for you given current conditions in your life. These goals reflect the state of your consciousness.

Here's some good news. If you feel strongly about a dream for your life, then natural gifts and skills will emerge to help you experience it. That dream is like a friendly eagle circling over your nest inviting you to fly with it.

Feel free to adjust your goals as you move forward in your life. Make sure you post your chart somewhere conspicuous, like on your bathroom mirror. This then becomes your vision, your roadmap to achieving your specific goals in life.

4 Why You Were Born

"The two most important days in your life are the day you were born and the day you find out why."

-Mark Twain

"Why were you born?" When I heard this question posed by hypnotherapist Sean Stephenson, I was intrigued. I had never considered it before. It resonated deeply within me. Don't we all, at some point in life, ask ourselves a version of this question? *Why am I here? What was I born to do? What is my purpose? What is the meaning of life?*

Rather than the job you do or the expectations you are trying to meet, the purpose of your life (and mine) simply is to be in the current moment and build a quality consciousness. This is the reason why we need to unbox ourselves. Unboxing ourselves is the chrysalis stage of personal evolution. Like caterpillars, we can choose to go into the chrysalis and explore what we will emerge as—who we truly are. This is the first step in our evolution. Once we are unboxed (have emerged from the chrysalis in a true from), we are ready to explore life as the butterfly we always were meant to be.

The universe leaves breadcrumbs everywhere for us to follow to find our authentic self in life. I saw my breadcrumbs once I had come to the point of feeling like I needed to "shed my old skin," like a snake. Though I was not miserable, or even particularly unhappy, I felt urgency to take a step in a new direction and evolve into the next, more authentic iteration of myself. I sensed I was going the wrong way. Then I had an aha moment that got me thinking freshly.

After meeting with the team at the U.S. headquarters of Coltene, a major dental products company located in Ohio, they invited me to speak to dentists about their Componeers product. I was excited to be part of this opportunity. Not only did it pay well and would give me a change of scenery, it was a fantastic ego boost. Officially going on the lecture circuit would be a critical step in becoming one of the top dentists in my profession. I liked the product. It was a fantastic new idea: prefabricated composite veneers that could immediately enhance a smile for patients at about half the cost of porcelain veneers. So, I said yes.

To begin the process, I was handed a long Power-Point presentation that was created by the dentist in Switzerland who was the inventor of the product. The lecture was very detailed, long and technical, and completely clinical and boring. It did not sound like my voice or resemble the way I communicated with my patients. After I watched this lecture, I decided to personalize it. My aha moment was the recognition that I wanted to help dentists lead happier, more successful lives, not just teach them to do better fillings.

The goal was to deliver the product information and get dentists to try the product, right? Keeping this in mind, I put myself in the seat of the dentists I would be speaking to and wrote the lecture that I would most like to hear. When the new lecture was drafted, it was completely different, only preserving a few facts from the original that I felt were important. The rest was about happiness.

I surprised myself. *Happiness?* I had used the song "Make Someone Happy" by Jimmy Durante as my opening theme and accompanied it by a montage of portrait photography of my patients rather than clinical closeups of teeth. The entire theme of the lecture was how to make your patients happy, and in turn, make yourself happy.

I loved delivering this emotional pep talk. Helping my patients find happiness had always been one of

my missions in my dental practice and now I was
empowered to help other dentists do the same for
their patients. That felt incredibly rewarding.

A surprising side effect of giving the lecture I loved
was that my presentations were the most successful
for Coltene. None of the other four speakers in our
lecture circuit had as much success with product
sales as I did, and I was not even trying directly to
sell the product!

My experience as a lecturer opened my eyes to the
fact that I love helping people find the spark in their
lives more than drilling their teeth—surprise surprise! Most successful dental speakers focus on the
clinical excellence of their care. I had chosen a completely different path: focusing on the emotional
needs of both the patients and the dentists. Something real inside me made me select this path and
take the risk to do it my own way, and it paid off.

The pursuit of happiness, joy, and passion subse-
quently become my new mission, and I began reading
books on happiness and watching videos of TED
Talks and movies on happiness. The more I learned
about happiness, the more I wanted to learn.

When you start focusing on something, you begin
seeing it everywhere. This also happened with my
happiness quest. It led me to begin to build a quality
consciousness and to trust the voice of my inner self
to guide me.

What Is the Meaning of Your Life?

Think for a moment . . . what would a meaningful life be like for you? Is it a Plan A life? Do you hope to, as Neale Donald Walsch puts it in the documentary *E-Motion:* "Get the guy, get the girl, get the car, get the job, get the house, get the kids, get the office in the corner, get the bigger house, get the bigger car, get more kids, get the grandkids, get the gray hair, get the sickness, and get the hell out."[1] Are you supposed to accumulate a lot of stuff that you cannot keep when you die? Are you supposed to gain a lofty title that demands respect from people you hope will admire you? A bigger house to hold more stuff? A showy car that makes you stand out from the crowd?

I certainly don't think so. To create a meaningful life, we need to listen to the inner voice, our conscious presence, and live in the moment.

When you have eliminated all the static that your mind likes to occupy itself with all the time, you'll be able to hear that voice.

There is a joke in spiritual circles that goes "You can lead a man to knowledge, but you can't make him think." Well, what a dilemma I had on my hands after my experience as a lecturer on happiness. I was a successful dentist who had just entered the lecture circuit and only had to follow this path a little longer to get on top of the dental game. In short, I was close to becoming the kind of dentist I had looked up to, and whose career path I had emulated until I attended the wedding in California—and this really scared the heck out of me.

As it turns out, success is addictive, regardless of how you achieve it. Achieving success while not pursuing your purpose is a curse that can devour you.

I had discovered a different path than dentistry, one that lit my fire and was not engendered by my ego. I was ready to pursue this path of teaching and speaking about happiness, pursuing your bliss, but making a transition was scary. This voice of my ego kept saying things like:

- "You have financial and family obligations. You can't risk changing your path as a hard-working dentist. It's selfish."
- "Life is not about your happiness. Keep your day job and later in life you can do what you want."
- "What will people think of you?"

What happened next was that I suddenly discovered other purpose-driven people all around me. These people stood by my side and became my new role models. Dentistry became more and more part of my vision rather than me becoming part of it.

In your own life, when this happens, you will no longer be attracted to watching programs like *The Real Housewives of Beverly Hills,* but rather to watching inspiring videos you would find on YouTube, such as one I saw of a couple that travels the world as part of their passion. You'll be attracted to other people with purpose, not only to people who excel at materialism.

The most beautiful thing about living a purposeful life is that there is no need to change what you do, only how you do it. Incorporating purpose into any career changes everything about it. Even if you are looking at a 180-degree career change after unboxing yourself, taking baby steps will make the transition easier.

If you have ever heard of the Law of Attraction, you will understand the next thing I am about to say. If not, then I recommend you watch *The Secret*, a documentary film by Rhonda Byrne that offers a synopsis of centuries of research into the phenomenon of attraction of like to like.

After I shifted my consciousness, I began to attract patients to my practice who wanted to have spiritual conversations with me. This worked out well for everybody. I got to learn about spirituality and my patients could distract themselves from the fact that they were sitting in a dental chair when they came to see me. The more my consciousness opened to the spontaneous purpose of life, the more information arrived.

The more I asked myself *Why was I born?* the more I discovered about my authentic self. In my case, it took a lot of peeling away of layers to reach my core—and I am always finding new layers to peel away. But I have made progress. I can now offer you a *feeling* of my "why" rather than a description. I feel I am a healer (of the soul), an inventor/problem solver, a soul that loves adventure/discovery, nature, and having the freedom just to be myself. I laugh at stupid movies, cry at the sad parts, and frequently have placed the happiness of others ahead of my own. Nature and water recharge my energy and deep inside I feel my consciousness pushing me on to a more spiritual path in life. I don't relate to sports talk, ego contests, or being "mature" very well, and prefer the goofiness of childhood any day. Music is magic to my soul. I love freedom, which according to my personal definition simply means being able to be myself and find contentment in every moment regardless of my circumstances. I love helping people in any way I can. Everything life has to offer, including material possessions, should be enjoyed with the right intent—in other words, if it makes you happy (your inner self, not just your ego), then get it, do it, or enjoy it.

In one simple statement: When people are ready, I can help them unbox themselves and live lives of greatness. Understanding this, I have switched my focus from exclusively fixing teeth to also helping people unbox themselves and finding their passion, gifts, and raisons d'être.

Now, I challenge you to explore your inner core and burn down your box, so you can escape the rat race and transcend to a life of purpose and love—just being you, whatever that means in any given moment.

We spend entirely too much time and effort trying to figure out our purposes. There literally are hundreds of books on the subject and if those were genuinely useful, we wouldn't need another. Still, I am here to give you one more opinion on what the purpose of our life is, just to add to the confusion.

The purpose of our lives, as I see it, is simply to do exactly what we are doing in this exact moment. That's it. So simple. You see, this moment we are currently experiencing is not accidental. Nothing is. This exact moment has been carefully planned by us, ourselves, to give us a learning experience. Every moment thereafter is the same. There are no accidents or coincidences. So, a more poignant question than "What is my purpose?" would be: "What is the purpose of a purpose?"

Are you confused yet?

Understanding that we are doing exactly what we are supposed to be doing, the challenge becomes trying to figure out why we are doing what we are supposed to be doing. Well, there also is a simple answer to that question! The purpose of a purpose is to build a quality consciousness. That is all.

In other words, every single moment has been planned to give us the opportunity to build a more quality consciousness, to help us make the right decision that benefits humanity as well as our spiritual selves, our consciousnesses, the real us. To boil it down even more, ultimately the goal is to make every decision based on love.

Many of us have spent years thinking about the purpose of life, our purposes. What are we supposed to be doing? The fear of not living our purposes is real and shared by billions of people, yet the answer is so simple: We are living our purpose every single moment. The beauty of life is that we are in complete control of our future and how we want to experience the purpose of our purpose. How we learn is not important to the Source, the Universe, or God (however you want to define it). Don't like your current classroom, your reality? Change it. Money, power, location, occupation, it all can change to your liking as we have learned in the infinite universe theory as well as the Law of Attraction.

Another great challenge many of us encounter is the notion of having gifts. Your gifts are the answer to the question of why you were born. Some of us have tried to figure out what special gift we have by which we could organize our lives, that special something we were born with that we must use or on our deathbeds we will feel as if we have missed out. The fear of living the wrong life or choosing the wrong life path is very real. But the prospect of this happening is an illusion perpetrated by your ego.

Let me give you a quick solution to your dilemma. We all have many gifts! You do not need to find one special gift that gives your life meaning because you are living your purpose in every single moment. You can always change what you do by using another one of your gifts at any time in your life!

Yes, change is good and necessary for growth. Furthermore, if you choose your direction, your occupation, and your life path based on what makes your heart sing, then you will be using your gift automatically.

Still confused about why you were born? Remember that life is all about trial and error. Make a list of about twenty things that you are curious about.

When I did this, I was curious about how consciousness is related to epigenetics, how the fractal patterns of growth (our circulatory system, trees, rivers, galaxies, and so on) relate to each other, and how travel bloggers make a living from their laptops.

Spend a little time looking at your list and try to figure out the common denominator. Is there an underlying theme? Narrow your list to a handful of items and then explore these in more detail. Play around with the concepts. Watch videos, webinars, read books, and surround yourself with people that share your curiosities. Over time something will stand out and that is what you then focus your energy on, your passion.

Want to take it one step further? Write down fifteen major problems the world is facing, such as hunger, and see how your newly found passion can be of service. The biggest challenges hold the biggest opportunity.

Using your passion to help solve the world's problems leads to fulfillment.

Now you can look for a golden business opportunity that uses your passion and gifts to do some good. How awesome is that?

5 STOP WORKING, START PLAYING

"If you do what you love, you'll never work a day in your life."

–Marc Anthony

As children, we knew exactly what we loved. The games, the toys, the sports, the people, the food—you name it, we knew. Why is that? Because our ego has not had the chance to develop to the point at which outside influences, social stature, and "fitting in" suppress and trump our own feelings.

Listening to the opinions and guidance of others is not the problem. The problem is that we stop listening to our own voices, our guts or intuitions. We begin to lose ourselves because we believe that others know better. The rationale is simple—we fear making mistakes, failure. And at a young, impressionable age, fitting in seems more important than finding ourselves.

Life would be significantly simpler if we followed our guts from the get-go.

Children and dogs have it figured out. Let me explain.

Almost everybody loves dogs. Why? It's because they love us regardless of who we are. They do not judge and they forgive quickly. Why? What is the big difference between them and us? They do not have minds like ours that are ruled by ego. Dogs do what they think is right or best to do now. They're spontaneous. We could learn a lot from them.

Children are not ruled by ego and will simply gravitate toward love. They will do what they love, eat what they love, and share what they love. Little children are innocent and loving, although society quickly changes this—unfortunately hate is a learned or taught behavior.

If we, as adults, could bring out our inner children and suppress the egos that shape our beliefs about ourselves, we could feel that love again. When we banish our inhibitions and fears of judgment, we become *unboxed* and free to *be* ourselves. What a novel concept.

All our lives we worked so hard to *make a living*. How about *building a life* instead? At some point in life, we begin to define ourselves by titles, such as

D.M.D., D.D.S., M.D., Ph.D., and job roles, like author, speaker, dentist, and accountant. Credentials and titles are designed to show how much more education or experience we have than everyone else. And sure, they can. A title can be used to define what we do, which helps us communicate. But when we expect more respect or to be treated better because of a title, then we are being ruled by ego. Ego leads us to strange and unhappy places.

Ego says:

- "I will not stay in this hotel room. Don't you know who I am?"
- "It's Doctor Smith, not Mister Smith."
- "You look awful, go change into something that looks more presentable."
- "Comb your hair, you know you don't look good like that."

These types of statements scream egomaniac. Let's not be that type of person. The more power we let the ego have over us, the less we will be able to understand who we really are and what we would really love to do, have, and be. If we let this situation go on too long, we can end up sad, angry, and lonely.

If you have forgotten what you love or what your true passions are, then think back to your childhood, before the ego took over. What did you do for fun when you were ten? What hobbies did you have?

What dreams? Dig deep and allow those feelings to come back up to the surface. You can still find your old passions and rekindle them, it's never too late. You also can and will develop new passion throughout your lifespan. Identifying your true self, your inner core, is a critical component to unboxing yourself and becoming free.

The magic in our lives begins once we identify and align with experiences we really love. You know what I am talking about—that feeling of warmth and excitement that overcomes us when we can't wait for the ensuing experience! We love to laugh, smile, and be goofy, weird, and human. The stuffiness we present to the world as adults is a fake front, a mask worn to protect ourselves from criticism (which, of course, bruises our good old egos). Once we drop the mask, we get back to the love. Discovering what makes your soul smile and shaping your identity around that will result in a happy life. As the adage goes, do what you love, and you will never work a day in your life!

Now if you try to blame your circumstances for things that are not going right in your life, think again. Everything we experience in our lives, every circumstance, is a direct result of our own creation. The mind leads, and the universe follows. This concept of creation is nothing new. Ponder this assertion Marcus Aurelius Antonius made in ancient Rome nearly 2,000 years ago: "The universe is change; our life is what our thoughts make it."[1]

We create our lives. Thoughts and perceptions create reality. Just remember, whatever life circumstance you find yourself in is part of your soul's life plan and you can change how you perceive it. How? By taking control of your "ship" mentally and emotionally. You are the captain of your life.

It's easy to get bogged down by comparing ourselves to more successful, better-looking, happier, or wittier human beings. No matter how high we climb the ladder of success, we will always be one rung below someone else. There is no best, only our personal best. How do we get out of a vicious cycle of comparison and misery? We identify how our ego is playing games with us and call it out. Recognize it.

Yes, it really is that simple. We need to identify the "I" behind the thinking voice in our heads, and instead focus on our consciousness. Once you take the power of ego away, your life will get easier.

We do not need to make millions to be happy. As a matter of fact, we don't need to make any money at all to be happy. We just need to *do* what makes us happy.

Most people feel they need money to buy stuff that then in turn will make them happy. But if you pay attention, you will easily realize that when you buy the new car, the new outfit, or the new piece of jewelry three days later the thrill is gone and you're not happy anymore. The ego would have you go chasing the next thing to fill the empty hole in your heart. But you don't have to fall for its tricks.

If stuff really worked, then the world would be filled with happy people, as we are a consumption-oriented society. All this the stuff we already own that we originally thought would bring us happiness now brings us the opposite, in fact, as we need to maintain, store, hoard, or guard it. God forbid we get dirt on that super fancy car. Who owns who? The car! We are slaves to our stuff, especially if we attach fictional value to it.

When we die, everything we own will either be worthless or sold so others have the cash to buy different stuff which they think will make them happy. We cannot take it with us and our stuff contributes absolutely zero value to our purpose here on Earth.

There is no virtue attached to material possessions. None.

Time is our most valuable asset. Creating lasting memories with our children, for instance, is priceless. No one can ever take those memories away. They do not require any maintenance and deliver a level of joy no material possession could ever hope to equal. Traveling and seeing this amazing planet can be done on a shoestring budget. If you do not believe me, read Rolf Potts' book *Vagabonding.*

Our occupations should be the furthest thing from a *job*. There are just too many ways to experience the adventure we call life for any of us to agree to spend most of it doing something we do not love. It is truly a sign of insanity. Unfortunately, this insanity is hammered into the heads of our children, with Plan A for their lives beginning so early that imagining a different option (Plan B) seems impossible.

Don't believe you can make a living traveling the world or doing something you love? Just head over to YouTube and see how many people are doing just that—and observe that they have millions of followers drooling over their videos because of how they had the guts to do what they love.

All it takes to become free is action—and the belief that anything is possible.

Because it is.

Chances are high that someone is already doing what you would love to do. There is absolutely no need to reinvent the wheel. Just research your passions and see what other, likeminded people are doing. Learn from them, follow their lead, contact them. Many would love to share insights from their journeys with you. Do not succumb to imaginary limitations that prevent you from reaching out.

My advice would be for you to pick something you would call a hobby and have an adventure. Do it for fun. As you focus on the opportunities out there regarding this hobby, you will gradually become aware of the ways that people make a living doing it. We can make our livings doing just about everything, including playing video games, shopping, traveling, exploring the jungles, and climbing mountains. The possibilities are endless.

Every career or job offers the opportunity to have fun. Yes, you can have fun doing just about anything. Work does not have to be soul-quenching labor all the time.

Find something about your daily routine that you can spice up, everyone around you will appreciate it. For example, bring coffee and pastries to a meeting, randomly smile at people and give them compliments, or tell terrible jokes and laugh at how bad they are yourself. Also, random acts of kindness throw people off and make them wonder why you are so happy. This is a good thing as it can inspire others to do the same creating a cascade of kindness. Think of the phenomenon of someone paying for the coffee of the person behind him at Starbucks, which then leads to many people doing the same thing.

You remember how to have fun. Just think back to when you were young. There is no law that says you cannot act like a child and have some fun at work. In fact, the opposite would be the foundation of a healthier workplace culture.

Another common misconception is that we need to pick a career for life. But this is simply ridiculous. There is no rule stating that once you've picked a career you are stuck with it. At any point in your life you can change course—it is, after all, *your* life. So, do what makes your heart sing and ignore any input from people doing things they do not like. Trust your intuition.

This world needs more happy, optimistic entrepreneurs who are constantly creating and evolving, not grumpy, unhappy realists who are following Plan A like good little lemmings.

With happiness being one of the fundamental goals of life, it is important for me to mention here that if you are happy living a life following all the rules, then what I am saying does not apply to you. Your life is yours and nobody has the right to tell you what you should be doing—including me! Your subjective experience of reality should be the only thing that matters to you. If you are not happy or fulfilled, then I hope my encouragement will give you the strength to make a change towards adding some fun into your daily routine.

Take action.

1. How serious is your life? How serious are you? You should have a pretty good idea at this point what your inner self desires. Do you enjoy a serious environment or a more relaxed one?

Consider your current work situation and think about how this environment fits you. Can you simply add some fun into this equation or will you need to make a job change? A circus clown would be a terrible employee at a law firm, for example.

2. Have you been living at the level of fun you really want, or could you use a daily dose of laughter? Do the people around you lift you up and make you smile or do they suppress your need for fun? Regardless of what you do for a living, are you surrounded by the right crowd? Sometimes it is not the job but the people that need changing.

3. Make it a point to do one thing every single day at work, for no less than one week, that will make you smile or laugh. Ideally, this would be accomplished by doing something for others or around others, so you can spread the positive mood. See what happens!

6 FEARLESSLY EXPLORE YOUR WORLD

The problem is that we think we have time.

Earth is not just a planet, it is our playground. That we can visit and explore nearly every corner of this amazing place is a gift to our generation from those who came before us. I challenge you to take full advantage of everything life offers through adventures and exploration, and to live with joy, compassion, gratitude, humility, and love. Life is short, so we must live it with passion and strength. But remember, you cannot authentically experience the wonders of the world if you are still living inside a box. Unboxing yourself is the first step to a free, amazing life.

Challenges in life are like stepping stones. Every day we face challenge after challenge after challenge. For instance, getting out of bed when we are tired is a challenge. Getting into the shower, getting dressed, brushing our teeth, and so on, are challenges too. We may not look at it this way, but they are.

If we were not used to brushing our teeth in the morning, it would be a challenge for us to find the time and motivation to do so. We would forget, procrastinate, make excuses, and do whatever it took not to brush our teeth.

Can't relate yet? Substitute *flossing* for *brushing*. Most people don't floss.

Every time we successfully complete a challenge, we have won a little battle against the entropy of the universe. Let's celebrate!

Do you have a bucket list—a list of things you would regret not doing if you were to die tomorrow? When will you begin to dig into that bucket?

What items will you have left in your bucket when you die?

What current scenario is more important than fulfilling the wishes and dreams sitting in your bucket?

Most of us don't have to dig very deep to get to some of the most common excuses for not doing fun things—which are work and time. The cold hard truth is that *we will never have enough time or money and life will only get more complicated.*

Welcome to the human condition. Procrastination is the dream killer that we all live with. Fear is the fuel for the procrastinator.

If you eliminate the fear of failure, you will notice that episodes of procrastination become less frequent. Embracing a few simple rules can dramatically improve your day-to-day task flow and help you to eliminate procrastination.

- If a task arises that takes two minutes or less to complete, do it immediately. Get it over with.
- Tackle the most uncomfortable tasks first, as freeing yourself of these results in the greatest satisfaction and can give you the energy you need to move ahead.
- Learn to say no to more tasks. *No* is a completely acceptable answer and one of the most powerful words in any language. No more doing of extra, unnecessary work. You do not need to solve everybody's problems and you do not need to take advantage of every opportunity that is presented to you.
- As much as possible, focus on *the one thing* that will make everything else in your life easier or unnecessary. For example, if you want to eliminate debt as your main goal then you could make your *one thing* to increase your income or pay off some debt each day.

Gathering information and gaining knowledge is important. We all benefit from those who have documented their experiences in different fields. But at some point, we need to stop the searching and act, just live our lives. We will never have all the information before it is time to make decisions. That is just the way the cookie crumbles.

The fear of making a mistake can be paralyzing. But nothing ventured, nothing gained. Be fearless.

7 LIVING IN THE NOW

"Some people are so poor, all they have is money."

–Patrick Meagher

There is no greater tragedy than ignoring the present moment because all we ever really have is now. Many of us lament at least a few events in the past that have affected us adversely and dream of a better tomorrow. We plan days, months, and years ahead, always expecting something to change for the better. We are emotionally invested in having a better job, better health, a better relationship, a better lifestyle—one filled with more pleasure and ease. We work so hard in planning for our future that we sacrifice our today.

When it comes to having the lives we claim we want, we are guilty of procrastination. We postpone vacations with our children due to the need to climb the corporate ladder so that we can make more money and *then* go on vacations, which we imagine as better, more glamorous vacations than the one we could afford today. We sometimes "go through the motions," but are absent-minded during birthdays, summer barbeques, holiday celebrations, and special events with our families because we are preoccupied with building a tomorrow that may never even materialize.

All of this is done mostly out of a good-hearted intention to do more for our families, friends, and ourselves. We derive satisfaction in being good providers and stalwart members of our communities, people who can be counted on to do the "right thing."

Having been a cosmetic dentist for much of the elite of our society for over a decade, I am thankful for what I have learned about life, happiness, and wealth. Becoming a dentist has not just been about fixing teeth. I strongly believe my career in dentistry has given me an opportunity to learn what life is truly about at a deep level. My dental patients have told me many stories about their money, relationships, and children, including many sad stories of pain and lost opportunities experienced by many wealthy people who you might guess "had it all" if you met them socially.

Due to my professional specialization, I usually meet high-achieving entrepreneurs and corporate officers when they are in their late fifties or early sixties, as this is when their teeth have been ground down to nearly nothing after decades of grinding and clenching, mostly due to stress. The initial consultation is always the same: I spend a few minutes sitting with them in a consultation room listening to a personal story. The two questions on my mind are: Why are they here now and how can I serve them best?

I can relate to the stress they describe, which is associated with constantly trying to grow, build, and maintain a business. It can become a never-ending struggle, if you let it.

Not only the teeth and smiles of my patients are worn down; so are their spirits. They are emotionally exhausted. The lines on their faces tell stories of pain that not even a forced smile could hide.

Coming to the dentist is a huge inconvenience for this type of individual, as they could be working and building the business empires that call to them 24/7 rather than taking a break to come see me. That's how I know seeing a dentist is important to them. Rebuilding their mouths and teeth so they can chew and smile again without embarrassment has been my bread and butter for as long as I can remember. What I have received in return for offering this service—and I am not talking just about money—has changed my life because it opened my eyes.

Rebuilding an entire smile takes time and allows me to get to know my patients well. Today, I would consider many of my long-term patients my friends. From them, I have learned about the toll that living for tomorrow at the expense of today can take on us in different ways. Let's explore a few.

Their Health Is in Jeopardy

Years and years of stress affect the entire body negatively. Human bodies are built to respond to stress with a quick and violent response triggered by the release of adrenaline. This is the fight-or-flight response. Think of it this way: You are sitting around a campfire and a bear shows up. You need to gather your strength quickly so that you can fight the bear, or else you need to run away at top speed to get to safety. Once the threat has been neutralized or you have escaped, you can relax. This is what the fight-or-flight stress response were designed for: to save your life in life-or-death situations.

Tens of thousands of years ago, this scenario played out occasionally and our ancestors managed to survive because of it; therefore, it is part of our innate genetic gifts. In today's world, life for most of us is much safer. Even so, sometimes we still face situations where we need either to fight or to run. But sometimes we feel stress and respond as if we're in danger when we're really not, such as while stuck in a traffic jam, repeatedly put on hold by a credit card company, or arguing with a difficult person.

There is a major distinction that separates our lives now from our ancestors lives in prehistory: In the modern world, stress never seems to end. We live in self-created stressful environments all day long that negatively affect the entire body.

Living with unending stress is a lot like driving your car with the gas pedal floored all the time. The engine's RPM gauge has a red warning line. If you hit that red line occasionally, your engine will be fine—you will feel a quick burst of power and then it will subside. But constantly running the engine in the red zone overheats the engine and can cause it to fail. The human body is a flesh-and-blood machine, and if we run its engine in the red "stress" zone, it will fail. We will get sick or even push ourselves toward death.

Patients of mine who have lived in the stress zone for too long are now experiencing the failure of their engines. Inflammation, one of the results of constant stress, begins to take its toll. Their joints are being replaced and they have heart attacks, autoimmune diseases, digestive issues, breathing issues, obesity, diabetes, emotional issues, teeth issues, and pretty much any other label doctors can apply to a failing body. Their health is a train wreck.

If you want to prevent the spread of inflammation and experience better health, then you need to focus on reducing stress. Stress, probably the most dangerous factor in the creation of overall poor health, and much of it can be overcome by unboxing yourself.

Stress takes a toll on the body by draining its reserves. Thus, another way to protect yourself from the effects of stress is to boost your reserves, for example by ensuring you receive adequate nutrition. Generally, there are many exceptional nutritional programs out there to choose among. Pick one and stick to it. You don't need to go to extremes to experience nutritional health, just select a program that you know you can live by.

Lastly, the body is designed to move. And movement is a great way to expel the tension caused by stress. You do not need to join an exercise "cult" to have a healthy body. Just using your body daily in some manner, such as by walking, riding your bike, running upstairs, and taking breaks from the computer or couch, can work wonders.

Their Relationships Are Failing

People who always put their business ahead of their relationships eventually will end up alone and lonely. The extra money they earn may provide them with a nice, cozy fireplace, but not much more. Few people who overwork year after year have meaningful relationships since they value their relationship with money above people. Many "rich" individuals have more money than they could want and nobody to spend it on or with who really cares about them. These are some of the loneliest people you will ever meet. Many are divorced, and often several times. Their connections with their children are superficial, especially if their children have elected to follow in their footsteps and become over-workers too. It breaks my heart to see how empty their lives become. To me, it seems that most of the relationships they have are with those who are seeking to learn how they "made all their money" and with those they hire to provide services. Such relationships fall short of being meaningful for the soul.

If you want meaningful, successful relationships with people, then you need to nurture them. Time is your most precious asset and you get to choose where and with whom you spend it. That which you spend time on will flourish because everything from a flower garden to a business requires attention. Friendships and relationships are no different. If you are always preoccupied with something else and are not being present in the now, then those living with you in the now will elect to find someone to hang around with who gives them the attention they want and deserve. You must focus on what is important and dedicate time and undivided attention towards that task or relationship.

They Have No Leisure-time Hobbies

If we don't cultivate the passions we discover in childhood, we forget them when we're adults. Sure, spending every waking hour building a business "empire" can result in a bigger empire, but at what cost? In the golden years, when these elite businesspeople have all the money they could possibly want, they often no longer have hobbies, passions, or dreams. Work has been everything to them, so they have few, if any, side interests.

You can play only so much golf. After golf, then what?

Retirement is a scary prospect when you don't have anything lined up to do. By the age when they should be looking forward to leisure activities, the bodies of workaholics are failing due to stress, so traveling and seeing our amazing planet is not as easy anymore. Therefore, they begin to stay home. What a waste of the most precious years of their lives!

If you want to unbox yourself, you must discover passions outside of your office and even your home. Everything eventually boils down to joy, passion, or love. What brings those three ingredients into your life? Do you love to read? Travel? Explore? Play chess? It does not matter what you do, so long as you do it.

As with relationships, time is required to nurture hobbies. These activities are your reward for whatever you do to earn a living. If you can make a living with your hobby, then you are way ahead of the curve. If not, that is fine, just pick something that you enjoy and make it a priority.

They Have No Sense of Purpose

Making a lot of money is not a purpose of itself. Yet, this is the primary objective of many boxed-in people—and their lack of true purpose makes them unhappy. They may talk about their financial wins and possessions, yet their lives lack meaning if they do not have something better to strive to achieve or experience.

What is the purpose of having all their stuff? Does it make them happy? It can be a struggle to maintain it. Based solely on how they spend their time, you might guess that their purpose is to be a slave to their stuff. Even worse, this purpose can never be fulfilled as they never feel that they have enough money and there is always someone with more money to whom they can compare themselves unfavorably.

Our purpose is to do exactly whatever we are doing currently. Accepting the present situation as it is and making the best of it is one of the most fundamental components of happiness. If we don't like the now we are living in, we can look back at how and why we created it and make a course correction for the future. We have no power over the now, but we have infinite power over the future—because the future is being created now.

It is critical that we completely accept our status and "own" it so that we change it to be whatever we desire for the next now, and the next now, and so forth. It never is too late to find a purpose that's bigger and more fulfilling than simply earning cash. If you don't know what that is yet, then perhaps your current purpose is to find your purpose.

We need to learn to laugh at ourselves and the crazy situations we dream ourselves into. It can be quite humorous to step back and look at ourselves and our self-designed boxes objectively. But then we must sit down, have a serious talk with ourselves, and create a plan to manifest something that's out of the box. Do this for yourself. Then, look at this plan daily, dream of it, get excited, and it will become your new and improved reality.

There is no past. There is no future. There is just now. That is how your mind responds to time and life. Becoming aware of this will give you more control over how you feel and react to everything. In every situation, you have options and learning opportunities. Accept the situation, decide what to do, and then live with the decision. You will manifest the future by focusing your mind and energy on creating more of what you truly want today.

8 YOUR ONE THING

"If you do not change direction, you may end up where you are heading."

–Lao Tzu

Have you ever made a snowman? If yes, then you know that every snowman starts with a small ball of snow that fits into the palm of your hand. Rolling this tiny snowball over and over in the snow covering the ground quickly results in a snowball so large that you can't move it. Like a snowman, every wonder in the world began within a single mind as an idea that grew until it became reality through the taking of a sequence of millions of small, daily actions—in essence, with the creator rolling the idea over and over in the landscape of the world.

We all have goals and dreams that seem so farfetched when we conceive of them that most of us don't bother to pursue them. But if instead of feeling overwhelmed we simply did one thing per day that brought us closer to our goal, no matter how big or small a thing it is, then it is inevitable that one day we shall achieve that goal.

A problem that can arise on the way to accomplishing a goal is that we take too many actions and lose our focus. To keep myself on task and avoid distractions when I am working on my goals, I carry a small magnifying glass in my pocket. I am easily distracted—kind of like the dog in the animated movie *Up* when he sees a squirrel. I chase my own tail and end up running in circles. Having something that reminds me to focus on the important things and not to deviate from them has been instrumental in keeping focused. A narrow focus helps me be productive.

Do you ever get super excited about all the opportunities you have and the amazing things you want to do only to become quickly overwhelmed to the point where nothing gets done? Having so much information, so many options, and so many choices can lead to information overload. When this happens, it's common to shut down and go back to what feels comfortable: the status quo. When this has happened to me, a natural fear of failure creeps into my mind that helps me to justify my inaction. That then spurs me to look for another book or website that has information to open me up to new possibilities, after which I get excited again and start the cycle over.

Focusing on finishing one task at a time, no matter how small or insignificant, has helped me break out of this cycle.

If you're like me in that you have moments of enthusiasm followed by inaction, the question is how can we break out of this cycle? Simple. Settle down. Don't try to take the entire world on in a minute. Just do take one step toward your goal per day. Focus.

Making even one small change in our routines today will change what we experience tomorrow. If you do so day after day you may find yourself surprised at how massively different your life is in even just a few months.

The first step is to be aware of your options and embrace the fact that you have a desire to change your life. If you identify with the struggle I outlined at the beginning of the book—of needing to get out of your box—then your first step will be to identify what makes you feel ecstatic. What makes your heart sing when you do it? It doesn't matter how big a thing it is, just be honest with yourself. That's the place where you can begin getting creative.

Choose one thing you love to add to your day to bring you closer to living as the person you really are. Peel back the layers of the onion of ideas that are covering up the truth. Work on including your one thing in your life more and more. You don't have to solve world hunger or cure cancer all on your own, just take one step closer to achieving your main goal. One thing.

The best way I have found to keep myself accountable for my intentions is to track my progress in a simple journal at the end of every day. If something is too complicated or requires too much work, then I just don't do it. In case you're the same way, I created a journal that you can download on my website www.drchrishahn.com/unboxyourself/journal. Make your own or use the one I made; it does not matter which. Just make sure you pick a way to capture your thoughts and that you are consistent in accounting for your actions.

A little daily progress works like compound interest in the bank. With the investment of one thing per day in the "account" of your future, growth is inevitable.

9 ENDING YOUR FEAR OF FRED

*"So many of us choose our path out of fear
disguised as practicality. What we really want
seems impossibly out of reach and ridiculous to
expect, so we never dare to ask the universe for it.
I'm saying, I'm the proof that you can ask the
universe for it."*

–Jim Carrey

Do you have a little voice in your head that tries to
sabotage everything you want to do? No matter how
prepared you are, this voice will try to make you
doubt yourself.

- "What if she does not like me?"
- "What if I fail the exam?"
- "What if I don't get the job?"
- "What if I forget my lines?"

Failure is so painful to the ego—which confuses it with *death*—that often we plan for failure, hoping to make it easier to swallow should it happen.

- "She probably won't like me anyhow."
- "I probably will fail the exam even if I study."
- "I probably won't get the job."
- "I probably will forget my lines."

If you are anything like me, then you know this voice very well. I know it so well that the voice and I are on a first-name basis. Its name is Fred. He tries to sabotage me so often that even my employees know who Fred is. Fred has a big ego and is terribly afraid of what people will think of him—or more accurately, what they'll think of me.

Over the course of the last year, I have learned to silence Fred more often, which has resulted in a new level of freedom for me. Perhaps *silence* is not quite the right word. It is amazing what happens when I don't ignore Fred but listen to him and accept his fear before realizing that it is not that important. Then I talk back to him and put him in his place.

"What if she doesn't like me?" —No big deal! There are many fish in the ocean and I want to be with someone who understands my crazy, unique self.

"What if I fail the exam?" —Worse things have happened! I will survive. Life is not defined by my performance on any one exam. My best is all I am expected to do.

"What if I don't get the job?" —There are millions of jobs out there! Once I find my passion and gift the right job or career will find me. Everything happens the way it is supposed to.

"What if I forget my lines?" —As if this has never happened to anyone before! Being able to be real and laugh at ourselves is a gift on its own. In life, all of us forget our lines much of the time.

Fear of failure can be debilitating. But Fred doesn't help us succeed—mainly he's a nuisance. One of the most important things I hope you take away from reading this book is that you should not be expected to live up to anyone else's expectations. Our world is yours to explore in any way or form you desire. You are the boss of you.

Nobody can make you feel anything. You are perfect as you are. So, whatever situation you find yourself in, remember that you put yourself there and you can change the conditions around you. Every experience has a purpose. It is a learning experience created by you to help you build a quality consciousness. You are a unique entity roaming this planet we all share, constantly working on becoming a better you. Nobody has this thing called life figured out any more than you do.

When Fred starts talking to you, how do you over-come the fears that are limiting your progress? I bet you know the answer already. You need to face those fears, accept what they show you, and then figure out what to do to solve the problem. Life goes on regardless of whether you succeed or fail.

Afraid to fail? Surprise, failure is an inevitable part of the learning process. Get used to it. Fail often and quickly.

Afraid of what others will think of you? Why? What power do they hold over you? Who are you trying to impress?

Embrace everything that makes you unique and it will help you to realize that you were not born to impress anyone or meet anyone's expectations. Your purpose in life is to explore your gifts and talents.

When you hear Fred's voice in your head, acknowledge the fear, counter it with a more positive idea, and move on. Fear has no power over any indi-vidual who chooses to replace it with a more positive emotion. If you can laugh when usually you would be embarrassed then you will have successfully have replaced the fear of "what other's might think" with humor, one of its most powerful antidotes.

Worrying does not make our lives any better. Worry only brings us down. Whatever problem or challenge we're facing, choosing to focus on steps we can take to find or create solutions will give us more energy and help us move forward. As the renowned reggae philosopher Bob Marley used to sing, "Don't worry, be happy."

What would the world look like if there had not been individuals before our time who overcame their doubts and fears to take creative risks? For one thing, the automobile and airplane would never have been invented. We might not have the television, electricity, modern medicine, computers, or mobile phones. People living the unboxed Plan B lifestyle learn to shift their focus.

In my own life, I have used this method of choosing a better thought to overcome many fears, including the fear of public speaking, the fear of failure, and the fear of criticism. At the point when you decide not to let Fred have power over you any longer life literally becomes a game of endless possibilities. Even the fears of having to achieve some sort of legacy or financial status vanish.

10 IMAGINE YOUR WORST-CASE SCENARIO

"Twenty years from now you will be more disappointed by the things that you didn't do than by the ones you did so. So throw off the bowlines. Sail away from the safe harbor. Catch the trade winds in your sails. Explore. Dream. Discover."

–**Mark Twain**

When everything in our lives is perfect, everything seems perfect. Life is simple. Life is easy. We are calm, happy, generous, and creative when life is going our way. But when, inevitably, something happens that is not ideal, how do we act and feel? Sometimes being challenged or facing obstacles brings out our character strengths. Sometimes aspects of our character that we are not as proud of are revealed when we do not get what we want. It's the classic Dr. Jekyll and Mr. Hyde scenario for most of us. And if the emotional back and forth is too frequent or extreme, it can affect every aspect of our lives from our relationships to our confidence. Life is filled with polarities: a beginning and an end, an up and a down, a plus and a minus, and so forth. This is the yin and yang quality of life. We would not be able to understand sound without silence. We will not understand the concept of rich unless we understand the concept of poor. Human experience is composed of pairs of opposites. The experience of painful emotions like anger and sadness enables us to appreciate how special love and happiness are.

To succeed and enjoy the good times, we need to learn to endure our failures and the bad times without unleashing our demons. We need to be able to remain stable at our centers as life swings its pendulum from extreme to extreme. Most of us would do just about anything to prevent ourselves from feeling the swing of the pendulum from good to bad. But trying to prevent ourselves from experiencing the natural flow of life only exacerbates our emotional reactions. Imagine gently opening a can of soda. There is a little pop as you open it up, followed by a small fizzing sound, and that is about it. That's what our response to life is like when we're maintaining a calm center. Whereas living reactively and feeling every extreme to the extreme is kind of like shaking the soda before opening it. By reacting to everything, it's like you are deciding to put the can of soda you're about to drink through some serious ups and down. If you shake the heck out of the can and then decide to open it, what happens? Yes, a huge monster mess is created as the soda explodes out of the can and splashes everywhere.

The moral of this story is that although you cannot prevent the natural flow of yin and yang, and may as well go along for the ride, you do not need to react to every experience as if it is a threat to your existence. Everything is cyclical in our world. Night and day, summer and winter, life and death. Everything. If you can remain focused on what you are purposely working to create and understand that all experiences are temporary, you will ultimately be happier and more productive.

When I was in high school, I participated in gymnastics. I had been a serious gymnast for the better part of my youth. One day a talent scout came up to my coach during practice looking for models for a Levi Strauss blue jeans advertising campaign. My body happened to suit their needs. Reluctantly, I went to the audition in Los Angeles where they made me try on dozens of different pairs of jeans in front of company representatives. There were a few other kids there who seemed to be having a good time. I was shy, however, so it was just as embarrassing to me as an audition for the reality show *Naked and Afraid* would have been. A few days later my mother excitedly told me I was selected as one of the models.

My first gig was going to be a runway show near the John Wayne Airport in Orange County. I sooner would have bungee jumped off the Eiffel Tower, but being a nonconfrontational guy who was too shy to complain, I went along with it. I could not have produced a better horror movie for myself if I had tried. It was a trial by fire because I had never done anything comparable before.

I arrived at the event, was ushered into a room with other models, and we were given a quick tour of the runway and told how to walk up and down it in a certain way. Then the event started. We paraded in front of dozens of industry leaders, wearing whichever clothes they asked us to while having our photographs taken.

I calmly walked up and down the runaway, then ran back to the dressing room to change in a hurry, repeating the process over and over and over. The good thing was that the stress of getting the correct jeans on and not being late for my turn was so high that I had little time to worry about how glowing red I must have been the whole time out of embarrassment.

To my surprise, I survived. And then I received a check in the mail a week later. Which I loved!

My mom saw modeling as an opportunity for me, and before I knew it I had an agent, a portfolio, and was attending weekly acting classes. This did not last long, of course, because of my terrible stage fright. I went on several auditions for commercials, but it was just not my thing, and I was glad when my agent stopped calling me about prospective assignments.

In my life, this is the best example of following the path of least resistance based on the opinions of others.

The ego is challenged by rocky times. It thinks we are responsible and that this makes us vulnerable, so it would push us to do almost anything to mask our involvement or change the outcome to one that fits its story of who we are supposed to be in a Plan A life. But we can unbox ourselves and escape the ego's pernicious grasp by not letting events define us.

One way to improve the quality of our consciousness is to do an exercise in which we imagine the worst-case scenarios we would face if our fears were realized. For example, if we unbox ourselves, what is the absolute worst that could happen? Would we face bankruptcy or public humiliation? Would our spouse want a divorce?

Once we identify whatever we believe the worst-case scenario will be and allow ourselves to accept this as a possibility, solutions will begin to present themselves. It becomes evident that there is life after every disaster. For instance, stories abound of how many successful businesspeople have gone bankrupt multiple times and been able to rebuild their finances. We see that the divorce rate is high. Many people have gone through one and found new partners afterward.

In every scenario, there is a path that already exists which we could follow if we needed to find a path. Yes, there may be temporary pain. But we can emerge on the other side of any problem happier and stronger. It is often a good thing, even if painful, to face disappointment and disaster because it helps us get clear about what matters and who we can trust to stick by us in times of need. Hard times can teach us about our character.

Much more is possible than is always evident to the human eye. Belief in possibility is an essential element of resilience when we are amid terrible circumstances. My mother taught me that as a child when I became ill—one of the worst scenarios she could imagine.

Right after the Christmas break from school when I was eleven years old and living in Bonn, Germany, with my parents and younger brother I noticed that my right knee was unusually sore. The sensation was like when you have a stiff joint for no reason as an adult, but I was young. I had neither injured my knee, nor was I sick. I didn't think much of the issue until a day or two later when I could barely move my knee. It really was not painful, which even to this day seems rather strange to me, but it meant I could not walk well—and the condition of my knee was getting worse. My parents took me to their doctor, who could not find anything specific wrong with me. A medical mystery had begun.

Surprisingly, I do not remember being worried, scared, or concerned about my knee. But maybe I have blocked this time in my life out. Now I only have glimpses of memories left of what happened over the next three months.

With the doctor not having found anything specifically wrong, I was sent home to rest and get better. Nothing got better, however. My knee locked up completely and then I also lost my appetite. I started to look sick and my parents really began to worry about me. I was taken to the local hospital where I underwent a barrage of tests. I had blood drawn so many times on my left arm that to this day I still get scared when I see a hypodermic needle. Every day I was handed a barrage of pills and liquid antibiotics to swallow. And to this day, the smell of liquid penicillin brings back memories so powerful that it is as if I am back in the hospital. I remember EKG tests and CAT scans being performed repeatedly, and doctors walking in and out of my room constantly. But not a single test revealed anything about my mysterious condition. Test after test, doctor after doctor, day after day, week after week . . . no answers.

If I had been getting better, or at least not getting worse, everything might have been okay, but I was getting worse. My right knee no longer was the only joint that was locking up—now my left knee was doing the same and walking, which had already become difficult, quickly became impossible. I had lost such a significant amount of weight that I looked like a member of the walking dead.

Within a couple of weeks, I was living in a hospital room full time. Occasionally, I was moved to a different room where I had a roommate—another sick child—with whom I could talk and play games. I saw the worry on my parents' faces when they looked at me. My mom visited me every day and stayed overnight with me in the hospital whenever she could. My school class also came to visit me one day and gave me a giant get well soon note that everyone had signed. That was a good day.

Two months into my illness, I was moved to another hospital that was closer to my family, so they could be with me more of the time. Nobody yet had any idea what was wrong with me. But the doctors treated me with antibiotics in case they would help.

The day I received a permanent IV portal on the top of my left hand is still a vivid, uncomfortable memory. It was a very painful experience. From that day forward, my hand was immobilized and everywhere I went I had to take the IV stand and the bags that hung from it with me. After that, all day long I would lie in my hospital bed looking up at the IV bag hanging to my left and watch drops falling from the bag into the plastic line that travelled down to the top of my hand.

Back in the 1980s, they did not have flexible needles, so my hand was Velcroed to a wooden stick to prevent me from moving or bending the needle on the end of the IV line. All I could do was lie there, watch the drip, and think. There was no such thing as an iPhone, a tablet, or another electronic gadget to keep me busy. I suppose I could have read more books. Instead I looked forward to such things as seeing the nurse come in and change my IV bag.

It is worth mentioning that you must quickly let go of your ego and learn humility when you are dependent on nurses for your care. Learning to use a bedpan is humbling, to say the least. You become completely helpless, like a baby again.

After about three months in the hospital just about everybody had given up on me. I had been to the best hospitals in Germany, seen specialists in just about every field, and still my parents and doctors had no answers. My body was skin and bones, a frame holding little muscle or fat. I could not walk anymore, and most people believed I would never walk again. The exception was one person: my mother. On the day that I was to be moved to a third hospital, one of my doctors brought me a wheelchair and put me into it. I was thrilled that I was mobile again. I remember smiling and being so happy, yet when I looked at my mother I saw that she was crying. I did not understand why. I did not know that the doctors figured I would be using the wheelchair for the rest of my life, however long or short it would be.

That day, my mother decided to stop believing in the doctors' expectations. She gave me a golden necklace and told me that it was a healing necklace that would make me better and I believed her. After that, as quickly as my illness had begun everything changed and I got progressively better.

While I was in the hospital, I do not remember spending a single day feeling despair, hopelessness, or sadness. I had complete confidence that my illness would pass, and I would be "normal" again soon because I believed my mother. She told me I would get better and better and better. Soon after she gave me the necklace, I went home. My joints healed and within no time I was my old self again.

Later, my mother told me that the doctors never knew what had happened to me but that they had told her I would never be able to do anything physical again, and if I ever walked again it would be a miracle. They told her sports were out of the question for me and that I was just lucky to be alive. Well, I defied the odds they gave and went on to become successful at just about every sport I played. As you know, in high school I was a gymnast, I ran varsity track, and I was an undefeated league champion wrestler.

To this day, I wear a similar gold necklace around my neck—the original was unfortunately lost—viewing it as a symbol of the power of the mind to heal the body and soul. When the challenges of life get the better of me, this necklace reminds me of something my mother has told me hundreds of times: *This too shall pass.*

What happened to me? I have no idea. I am convinced it was a lesson for my parents as well as for me. Fortunately, I was sheltered from the emotional aspects of this illness by God, Spirit, Source, and my mother.

I am thankful that I have not had to experience this type of worst-case scenario with my health again. But I have experienced others. Looking back on each one, I can see a lesson in it. My *shift* to leading a purpose-driven life happened not that long ago.

Unboxing myself opened an entirely new world to me. It took a lot of pressure from the universe for me to finally wake up to the abundant possibilities that lay around me. And since I did, each day has been easier and more peaceful than the day before.

These days, I live in my center and can sustain my equilibrium no matter which way the pendulum is swinging. Negative people have little to no effect on how I act or feel. Fear doesn't stop me from acting on my desires and instincts. That, my friend, is freedom.

The ultimate worst-case scenario for all of us? *Not* finding yourself and living a life of regret, then taking your last breath realizing you let fear dictate your life instead of passion.

The insignificance of our daily problems becomes crystal clear to us whenever we are faced with the consequences of our mortality. But why does it have to take death or the fear of death to wake us up? Must we go through severe challenges and heartbreaks to overcome our complacency? I do not know. Now, in my forties, I am fed up with the daily grind and feel the clock ticking. There is a clear fear of not living the life my soul desires me to live, and this fear is driving me to make drastic changes in my life.

Have you reached a point in your own life where you are afraid you will fail to live up to your full potential? It is not a good feeling. Realizing that the worst-case scenario is living a life of regret may help you make good decisions that lead you to live a life you can look back upon with great satisfaction on your deathbed.

What are the worst-case scenarios you can imagine for your life? Write down several versions and make them all terrible. Make them very, very bad. Once you've written your descriptions, study them, read them, think about them. And ask yourself questions, like: Has anyone else ever dealt with such a disaster? Are they still alive? Are they thriving?

Most likely the answers will be, yes, they faced it, they survived it, and they are thriving. And you will too if your worst-case scenario comes true.

Will it take a little time? Yes, it most likely will. But so what?

After I write out a worst-case scenario, I find it helpful to write out the options I would have if I needed to face it. What would I do? What would I need to change to take full advantage of the opportunity to restart? It makes me feel freer just thinking about how many options there are.

Continuing to live inside a box is one of the worst-case scenarios I have imagined. Think about your life and what will happen to you if nothing changes. Would this be a good scenario for you? I bet that doing nothing is not your best option either. Use this exercise and the principles in this book to discover new options.

11 ACT ON YOUR INTENTIONS

"If you want to be successful, you have to jump, there's no way around it. When you jump, I can assure you that your parachute will not open right away. But if you do not jump, your parachute will never open. If you're safe, you'll never soar!"

–Steve Harvey

Information is a wonderful thing to have, and completely useless unless it's implemented. Which is why every motivational speech contains an action statement. I am sure you have heard these platitudes as many times as I have.

- "How do you eat an elephant? One bite at a time."
- "Nothing happens if nothing happens."
- "From nothing comes nothing."

These self-evident statements are true. We cannot get anywhere in our lives without taking steps. Seriously, think about it. Unless we get out of bed, we stay in bed. Unless we get dressed, we walk around naked. Unless we pick up a fork and put food into our mouths, we don't eat. We are pure action figures all the time! Our survival depends on our actions. Without action, none of us would even be here. So, why are we afraid to act in ways that could only benefit us? Simple. Because we overthink the actions we must take and procrastinate.

Our minds are awesome tools, but they can also completely overanalyze, dichotomize, judge, scrutinize, bifurcate, and basically confuse us *ad infinitum*.

Here is a scenario: You are taking a leisurely walk in the park and before you can blink a baseball comes screaming toward your head. How much thinking will you do before you duck to avoid getting hit? None! You will quickly move your head without even as much as a single thought.

That is the type of action you need to take once you perceive something you desire to do. An immediate, instinctive, reflexive action.

Now, if you were to treat the scenario with the baseball like you made a recent *decision,* perhaps analyzing all the possible outcomes for days, you would get smacked directly in the head by the baseball, wouldn't you? Conscious thought is slower than reflex.

My point is that life is not much different than that scene in the park for any of us. Daily we are bombarded with "objects" that require us to make quick decisions, not engage in deep analysis. We need to avoid "paralysis by analysis" —that's one of my favorite aphorisms. Somehow when we are given the time to think things over we usually mess things up. Too many options can lead to no decision at all, whereas knee-jerk responses are often quite accurate and helpful.

Self-improvement is a popular topic people like to study. I myself have read so many self-help books that my consumption borders on the ridiculous. What exactly are we looking for in those books? The magic formula? The secret to life? The perfect path? You may laugh because, if you are like me, then all the above is true. Nobody wants willingly to make a mistake. The main reason I read these books is that I feel there is some information in there I must have or else I will make a mistake. Fear of making mistakes is a leading cause of procrastination. "Collecting" information is useless without implementation and action.

Why not wait until we have all the information we can amass and then decide? Frankly, because we will never have all the information. We need to make decisions quicker, before the "balls" that life pitches in our direction hit us in the face.

In my estimation, all we really need is 75 percent clarity before an appropriate decision can be made that leads to our next powerful action.

Making mistakes is human, and an essential component of the learning process that ultimately makes it possible to be successful and achieve our dreams. Note that I said *achieving*, not *receiving,* our dreams. You need to earn your success or else it will be worthless to you. The struggle involved in achieving our dreams, the journey, is the real reward because the necessity of meeting a challenge teaches us so much about ourselves—both our strengths and our weaknesses. Our true character and underlying beliefs and capabilities are revealed when the shit hits the fan.

If you don't believe me, consider the statistics on lottery winners. They are handed their dreams, yet never get to experience the reward of the journey of success. The house, the car, and the stuff has significantly less meaning if you have not earned it yourself. Consequentially, most of them are either broke, miserable, or both within a short period time. The children of the ultrawealthy suffer the same fate. Many are bored out of their minds and depressed because they never face any obstacles to overcome.

Here's a more personal example from my past. One year my brother wished for a train set for

Christmas. He was very excited about the prospect. The ability to create any landscape you desire, build a train to run through it, and essentially bring to life a miniature world through your imagination? Extraordinary! My brother was around eight years old and my father loved giving us what we wanted all the time. (This was done out of love, but in retrospect I see it as a mistake.) So, my father went out and bought a very expensive, completely built, large train set that was set permanently on a huge table in our house.

My brother's train set was awesome, a work of art. It had mountains, trees, cars, tunnels, everything you could want in a train set. It was completed and ready to run. Somebody had spent months, if not longer, building this masterpiece and when my brother received the gift he was thrilled . . . for about an hour. He sat down, pushed the lever, and watched the train run around the landscape, through the tunnel, up the hill, and back. But there was nothing for him to do beyond admire it. The painting was complete, the art project over, the fun had vanished. He never played with the train set again and never again expressed any interest in trains. His dream had been destroyed.

Looking back at it now, it was a very sad moment. Something similar happened several times in our youth. Bigger is not always better. The fun is in the journey, the adventure, the ups and downs, the failure, the learning, the achieving, the earning, and *not* in the receiving.

Acting despite the possibility of failure is courageous. Knowing that we will probably fail many times in different ways before we achieve success makes success sweeter once we accomplish our goals. Still going for it is despite the inevitability of periodic setbacks is what creates champions. Thomas Edison invented the light bulb after over a thousand attempts. That is a lot of failure to endure, yet his final product changed the world, so it's a good thing he did!

You want to be propelled forward by your passions and skills. So, action it is. Daily, calculated action that moves you toward your goal. How I wrote this book is a demonstration of what I advise. I have always wanted to write many books. Then I realized how much work goes into writing one good one. Hours, weeks, and months of writing go into even the shortest well-written book. It takes a lot of action.

So how would I write my book? Many people spend so much time trying to find the perfect title that they never get passed that initial hurdle. I picked a title and moved on to the next action step quickly, knowing I could always change it later. Then I made a commitment to write something every single day, even if it was just a single sentence. I knew that if I did not take daily action then it would never happen.

It was not easy finding time to write something meaningful every day, but before I knew it the book was completed. I loved the challenges of writing and my love for inventing solutions to those problems helped me stay on track to achieve my publishing goals.

Finding a daily dose of motivation is part of my routine. I use the inspiration that others share as they move through their journeys to help me stay on track with steps toward my own goals. One of my all-time favorite quotes comes from Les Brown. He says: "The graveyard is the richest place on earth, because it is here that you will find all the hopes and dreams that were never fulfilled, the books that were never written, the songs that were never sung, the inventions that were never shared, the cures that were never discovered, all because someone was too afraid to take that first step, keep with the problem, or determined to carry out their dream."[1]

Imagine that you wake up in the morning next week, and as you get ready to take your shower you run into a large, dark figure in the hallway that gestures you to come closer. You reluctantly comply and quickly realize it is Death in person. Death looks at you and calmly says it is time to come with him and leave Earth. You look at Death and say with desperation: "Death, I am not ready! I still have so many things to do! I am only fifty (or whatever age you are) years old! Can you please give me another week?"

Death replies: "I am sorry, I cannot give you another week, I already gave you fifty years." And off you go.

If Death came to you tomorrow, would you be ready to go and put your stamp on a life well lived or would you have regrets? Are there people you need to forgive, relationships you need to nurture more, places you still want to explore? Adventures you want to undertake? What if Death gave you an extra week? How about an extra year? What if you had several years left? The mystery is not if Death will come for you—because you already are on the schedule. Your time has been determined and it may be today or fifty years from now.

If you died today, what dream would you take to your grave? Would your life have been worth living? What regrets would you have? Knowing there's a contribution you have yet to make, which your soul is aching for you to make, what action steps could you take today? Tomorrow? And the day after that?

There is only one solution to the problem of death: Live each day as if it was your last on earth. Think about your life, your purpose, and make the necessary changes as soon as you can! Tell people you love them. Call or write your friends and family and tell them how they have impacted your life and thank them for it. Share a smile with someone going through a rough time. Also shed material responsibilities that are burdening on you and focus on living a purpose-driven life. Improve the quality of your consciousness.

Also, take daily action so that when Death comes for you, you can smile, thank him for the time you were given, and willingly take his hand and return to your spirit form to get ready for your next adventure.

I challenge you to make those changes today. To chase your dreams, take risks, and lead a life full of adventure and wonder. Discover the difference between living and existing, then pick what you do carefully. In the words of Steve Harvey, "Jump!"

12 RAISE YOUR VIBRATION

"Keep away from people who try to belittle your ambitions. Small people always do that, but the really great make you feel that you, too can become great."

–Mark Twain

Misery likes company. Everywhere you go, it is easy to identify people who flourish by spreading negative energy. *Negatoids.* How many of your friends love to spread the latest gossip they have heard? Ever hear a group of people going back and forth in their discussion on who has the most medical issues? It is easy to fall into the trap of surrounding ourselves with negatoids and living from one tragic news story to the next: terrorism, global warming, drugs—the list goes on and will never end. When was the last time you watched the evening news and heard a positive story? Negatoids love to discuss and worry about worst-case scenarios.

We need to make an active decision to quit the negativity club and form friendships with individuals who choose to be optimistic, hopeful, and happy. As soon as you make this decision, you will begin to see an entirely different world. We become what we think about and mimic those with whom who we surround ourselves. Eliminating negative influences, such as bad news programs, people listening to and spreading gossip, and most importantly negatoids is a critical step in developing an optimistic attitude in life.

Here is the hard part. Many of our friends, even family, are part of the negativity club. Some of them we have known for nearly all our life. Limiting the negative impact these individuals have on us can be challenging and requires us to slowly reduce our exposure to them. No small task but it is an essential step towards freedom.

We all try to surround ourselves with like-minded individuals. When one member of our peer group decides to move beyond the perceived limits of the group's conventions, it is often regarded as a threat to the group's emotional security. The unknown scares many people, so when you decide to be different, such as being a positive individual who does not proliferate negative thinking in a gossipy social circle, then you risk the possibility of being shunned by your pack. This is the point at which you will need to seek out new acquaintances and surround yourself with individuals who welcome your growth and encourage your dreams.

They do exist, I promise.

Every aspect of our lives is measured against what we know and consider possible. If you are in a pack where the most successful individual earns $60,000 per year, then that is your goal and measure of success. In another pack, the high earner makes $6 billion per year, making that the goal. Do you think the high earner making $60,000 per year would feel the same level of success in the pack where the high earner makes $6 billion? Our limits are set by our imagination, which is only as big as our pack allows.

Finding a group of individuals to surround yourself with that see you as the limitless being that you truly are is critical if you are to reach your full potential. Growth requires a positive, "You can do it" attitude. Negatoids will shoot down your attempts at greatness every step of the way due to their own fear of failure, not yours.

Who we associate with in all aspects of our life is critical. It has been said that we are the average of the people we surround ourselves with every day. Look at it this way. If you take a pot of boiling water and combine it with a pot of freezing water, you end up with lukewarm water in a few minutes. Everything evens out. It does not matter how warm or cold the two pots of water are, they will combine to form an average mixture.

Groups of people are the same. Spend enough time in a group and you will adapt to its limits quickly, regardless of how hot or cold you were at the start. Packs exhibit similar opinions, likes, dislikes, goals, dreams, and so forth. Anyone who tries to introduce new ideas to a group that prefers negative, limited thinking most likely will be a threat to the stability of the group and, as such, be pushed out. Each of us needs to take a close look at our pack, who we surround ourselves with, and if this is a limiting or unlimiting group of individuals. Is our pack stuck in a rut or focused on the negative vibrations in life, or do they always view their glass as half full?

Positive people lift you up and always look for the good in everything. They can really annoy a negatoid. Find as many positive people as you can and make an active effort to be around them as much as possible. Find those who have happy, respectful relationships, big dreams, and never seem to stop smiling. High energy is contagious and just like the hot and cold water, you cannot help but be lifted by these individuals. Surround yourself with high energy, optimistic, happy people and watch how contagious their positive energy is.

The second component to this is of course to eliminate the negatoids from your life, as they drain your
life energy. As soon as you stop feeding their negative
energy habit, they will pull away from you and seek
another victim to drain. There are plenty of victims
out there.

Once you have identified your passion—you know,
that thing that lights you up when you begin talking
about it—you will need to find people who share this
passion and have already committed their lives to it.
Surround yourself by these people and watch how
you are elevated by their positive energy. Just like
the case was with water, where the cold water is
brought up to a higher temperature just by being
surrounded by hot water, your vibrations will begin
to rise and mimic those of the people you are around
most of the time.

For example, let's say you want to become a motivational speaker. Many of your friends always tell
you that you would make a great speaker. You read
many books on the subject and have the energy to
support the career, yet you still are not a motivational speaker. You do not know where to start and
making a career change is scary. How will you make
any money? How will you pay your bills? What if
you fail? There are just so many bad variables that
you are paralyzed with indecision, and for this reason

you have not and will not move forward. What do you do?

First, work on your energy. Your vibration needs to be corrected. All your worries will not move you one step closer to your goal. You need to surround yourself with people with the right vibrations. Among other things, this means finding people who already make a living being a motivational speaker. Also, find a mentor. Develop relationships with motivational speakers. Make it a point to communicate with them more and more, at least daily, until your life slowly begins to shift toward resembling theirs and your vibrations match.

13 SIMPLIFY YOUR MORNING ROUTINE

"If you want to change the world, start off by making your bed."

–Admiral William McRaven

One thing that I have learned over the last few years is that successful people have daily routines that help them act. I never was one for establishing a good routine until I began evaluating my life and realized that there were too many random variables in it.

None of us can multitask, even if we think we can; this has been proven again and again. So, let's be realistic and acknowledge that when we try to do ten things at once we are setting ourselves up for failure. Daily routines that reinforce good, monotasking habits help us to calmly focus on the most important things in our lives. That's how we can achieve the snowball effect in several areas at a time.

A poor approach to time keeps us trapped in a box. Too often our minds are cluttered with chatter that obstructs our ability to get anything done. We try to hold our to-do lists, ideas, and worries in our conscious minds throughout the day and juggle tasks in hopes of not dropping any of these balls. Then, nothing gets done correctly or fully and our stress level makes the day a burden rather than an adventure.

Here's how it happens in my life. I am an idea hoarder. Step one to help me clear my mind is always to identify the problem. Currently there must be four or five small notebooks floating around my house that I have labeled with phrases like *Ideas* and *Inventions*. I also use an app to keep notes on my smartphone. I keep these notes because I know that whenever I have an idea for a business or product I need to write it down or I'll forget it. At the time of conception, every idea seems to be better than sliced bread. The newest idea quickly takes the forefront on my to-do list. I will then go online and register several domain names where I could build out a business page for it.

If you ever have a good idea and try to buy the domain for your business only to find it is not available, then someone like me probably has bought the name and is sitting on it.

My behavior is habitual rather than effective. There is no clear routine or process to this madness. As a matter of fact, it is expensive and very distracting. It pulls my focus away from the things I have previously committed myself to doing which are earning me a decent income and securing my family's well-being, including my established business. I hoard these ideas and execute very few.

This pattern has gone on for years now; and while I have had some pretty good ideas and have even sold some patents and built some companies, overall the time and money that goes into constant idea generation is not worth the stress it creates for me. There needs to be a system, or a routine, that would help me manage this process better.

You probably have your own thing like this, something that takes up a lot of your time and gives back little in return. A *time thief,* if I may coin a phrase. Is it social media? Collecting posts/photos? Trinkets? Most of us hoard something and spend a lot of our day "hunting" for it.

Once I recognized this poor routine, I decide to find a reminder that would help me change it so that it would not consume my attention and interfere with the more valuable aspects of my life. I now carry a small magnifying glass in my pocket that is covered by a little leather sleeve. Inside that sleeve I wrote the number *one* in permanent ink. Every time I put my hand into my pocket and touch this magnifying glass, it reminds me to focus on the one thing that will make everything else easier or unnecessary.

This is a practice that I adopted after reading *The One Thing* by Gary W. Keller.

On the other side of the leather sleeve, I wrote the word *now* to remind me to focus on living in the moment and address the lesson each obstacle I face is teaching me.

Creating positive, productive routines and mnemonic devices to wake us up to what matters helps us clear our minds so that we can focus on the important things in life, such as unboxing ourselves.

If you stop spinning your wheels, focus on the one that thing that will help you get closer to your goal in the moment, and then do just that one thing, you will soon burn through the list of items that it is necessary for you to do to get to where you want to be. If you cannot tell what your one thing should be at any given time, then finding out what your one thing is must be your highest priority that day or moment. It really is that simple.

A good daily routine supports you in following through on your intentions. This is where your purpose gets broken down into baby steps. Making aspects of your daily schedule, such as waking up, showering, brushing your teeth, exercising, and eating healthy, into a routine takes away some of the stress of the morning and allows you to start the day off right. If you wake up in the morning and everything that you need to get done floods your mind and you don't know what to do first, then you have already lost. If instead, you wake up, smile, take a few deep breaths, and thank the universe/source for providing you with another awesome day, then you are setting the stage for a positive experience.

How can you establish a good daily routine for yourself? If you are anything like me, especially how I was until a few years ago, you will want to create a *perfect* daily routine. You will research Tony Robbins and other significant motivational speakers and try to figure out what they do, because they must have the *perfect* daily routine, right? Wrong.

You are not them. They created personalized morning routines that work for him. And you must create the one that works best for you. Be experimental and keep tweaking it until it is ideal for your needs.

Yes, of course I researched Tony Robbins' morning routine. But jumping into a bath of freezing cold water as he does is not yet on my short list!

There is nothing wrong with researching daily routines; it is a fascinating subject. Until I did this research I was unaware of the fact that most people already have routines, good and bad. There were many similarities in the morning routines of successful, happy people. They usually involve meditation, affirmations, expressions of gratitude, and reviewing points of focus.

By contrast, unhappy people commonly hit the snooze button continuously, watch the negative news and dive into their social media accounts, all which fill their minds with negative information.

In my experience, there are few things in the world as powerful as a positive routine. This is my current morning routine:

- The first thing I do when I wake up I say thank you to the Source, for another amazing day. Thank you for giving me the gift of life and the guidance to live my purpose. Thank you for this moment and helping me live in the now. Then I smile.

- I immediately roll out of bed and head into a short, warm shower. I do not do the cold shower technique so many people enjoy (finishing your shower with a few seconds of cold water), as I have enough energy as it is. In the shower, I think about how amazingly good the hot water feels on my skin, how lucky I am to be able to take this warm shower, and what great things will happen for me on that day. I go through a list of things I am grateful for and spend a minute or two meditating on my breath. I take deep breaths in through my nose on a count of two to three seconds, hold the air in my lungs for three seconds, then exhale it through my mouth on a count of five seconds while relaxing every muscle in my body.

- Following the shower, I walk to my closet, look at my affirmations and life vision statement posted there on my vision wall, and quietly say them aloud to myself. I then come up with three things I am grateful for that day and three things with which I would like some help or guidance.

- I sit down on the floor in my closet, stretch a little, and then get dressed for the day. Usually my cat and dog are there with me, vying for my attention.

- Next, I head to the kitchen. I feed the animals and make my first cup of coffee—another of my favorite parts of the morning. The house is quiet because no one else is up yet. I spend ten to fifteen minutes listening to a guided meditation audio, or otherwise focusing on my consciousness and asking for guidance from the Source to help me live in the now on that day. I sit there for a good thirty minutes, sipping my coffee and writing in my journal. At 6:30 A.M. sharp, I wake the kids and the chaos of the day begins. I let my wife sleep in.

My morning routine varies a little from day to day, but essentially this regimen is what I shoot for. Thirty minutes of peace and me time, at a minimum.

To paraphrase Tony Robbins, if you can't find at least ten minutes of "you time" each morning, then you don't have a life. A quality life.

Everybody needs to create a simple morning routine that works for them. There is no right or wrong routine, only the one that works best for that individual. Just make sure you are being authentic to your own needs and values. In the end, it's all about what works for you.

You don't need to overthink this routine. You can adjust and change it anytime. As you practice your routine, I am certain you'll discover for yourself that how you spend the first hour of each day sets the tone for the rest of your day. You shouldn't blindly believe me, or anybody for that matter. Test what I am saying and come to your own conclusions.

Admiral William McRaven, who in his now-famous 2014 University of Texas at Austin commencement speech said, "If you want to change the world, start by making your bed,"[1] outlines the importance of a strong morning routine and beginning each day having accomplished one task already. I personally have researched many successful individuals, and so far, nearly all I studied have clear morning routines involving the concepts he outlined: meditation, gratitude, exercise, and healthy eating.

Keep it simple but, by all means, develop your own strong morning routine.

14 PERFECTLY IMPERFECT

"Striving for excellence motivates you; striving for perfection is demoralizing."
–**Harriet Braiker**

Let me share a struggle with you that I have had all my life in the hope that it will help you overcome some of your struggles. I struggle with perfectionism.

What is a perfectionist? And shouldn't a cosmetic dentist be a perfectionist? How could that be a bad thing?

All my life, I have chased perfection. Nothing I did ever seemed good enough. As far back as I can remember, I expected myself to achieve whatever I put my mind to, and most of the time I was able to. When I did fall short, such as when I received a failing grade on a test in fourth grade, I felt panic. To this day, I remember receiving a grade of six out of ten on that test and feeling fear while I was running all the way home from school. I don't remember telling my mom what happened, but I still can recall the image of myself with my backpack on running as if I was being chased by a bear.

"The fear of failure is strong in this one," as Yoda might say.

Where did this fear come from? I honestly have no idea. Perhaps it was a byproduct of the months I spent in the hospital unable to walk or of my training as a gymnast. I had high expectations of myself, even higher expectations than my parents. Of course, my parents expected me to study and do well, but I do not recall them ever harping on me about getting "perfect" grades. They paid me an allowance for my grades and good grades were worth a lot more than bad grades, but that does not seem motivation enough to drive a child to extremes or provoke anxiety.

The fear of failure that has haunted me all my life resulted in me always working and studying hard, which enabled me to succeed in school, and then business, most of the time. When I became a gymnast at age eight, I did well, but I never felt successful. I was sick for most of my eleventh year. When my family moved to California from Germany, I was age thirteen and I learned English within six months, managing to get on the honor roll that year. Still, no satisfaction. Somewhere along the line, at an early age, I lost the ability to feel fulfilled or like I had achieved anything at all.

Let me elaborate. Every challenge in life, whether a test, a class, a gymnastic routine, a race, was a complete letdown at the end. The first time I realized this was in high school. I was a good student. My GPA was above 4.0, and I graduated as the class valedictorian. On the wrestling team, I was the undefeated league champion for my weight class. I was also voted the most valuable sprinter on the varsity track team. Everything was going according to plan, until graduation. Then the challenge of school was over, and I felt flat.

At the graduation ceremony, all my friends threw their caps in the air and were genuinely thrilled to have achieved this educational milestone. I, on the other hand, felt more embarrassed and self-conscious than excited. To me, in my head, this challenge was not worthy of such celebration. *Everybody can graduate from high school,* I thought. *So, how is that a major milestone? How is that worth celebrating?* I did not want the attention this celebration was drawing to me and it felt very uncomfortable.

What would it have taken for me to feel like I had achieved something truly worthy? The presidency? Now, decades later, I believe the answer does not lie in a larger accomplishment, but in changing my focus.

After high school, I went to college and continued striving for perfection in my studies. At the University of Southern California, as an undergraduate, I was one of just two students who were admitted into dental school without an interview. I also only had two years of education under my belt and no degree yet. Looking back at this now, I can see that I should have been thrilled, proud, and excited, but I expected it, so the achievement had little luster for me.

Throughout dental school, I also was one of the top students. I graduated magna cum laude, meaning "with great distinction." At graduation, everybody had to wear fancy robes that made us look like judges or monks. I felt overdressed.

At the end of the ceremony, we were asked to move our tassels from one side of our caps to the other, signifying we had graduated. After doing so, most of my classmates tossed their caps in the air in celebration, just like they did at my high school graduation ceremony. Not me. I was a little excited, but already looking for the next adventure, which was securing the best job I could. I always seemed to miss out on the excitement of the moment because I was looking for the next big thing.

When would I find the top, the magical achievement that would give me satisfaction I sought and allow me to sit back, relax, and say to myself, *You did it?* Would it ever happen? It didn't seem as if I would ever learn to stop and smell the roses. The pursuit of perfection followed me everywhere. For years, I proudly told my patients I was a perfectionist—which was true—and they approved. I put incredible effort into every dental restoration I placed, every tooth I touched. I wanted everything to turn out perfectly. And of course, I continue to take seriously my obligation to do excellent work on the teeth of my patients. The difference is that I am not driven by false concepts of perfection anymore.

My USC Dental School education was amazing. Every day I still try to live up to their high standards. Having been in the field now for almost two decades, I can appreciate the level of excellence they expected. What an incredible dental school. With every filling I placed, every crown I delivered, I tried to live up to my instructors' incredibly high expectations. There has been only one time where I felt I compromised, knowingly, a little. I was cementing a gold crown where one of the edges was just not perfect. Every time I saw that patient my heart sank until I could no longer take it and remade the crown.

Was the original a terrible crown? No, it was acceptable by most standards. But it drove me crazy because I failed when I tried to accept average results.

My dental practice flourished because I loved interacting with patients, helping them and delivering premium quality care. To take dentistry to the next level, I then became one of the youngest, if not *the* youngest, American Academy of Cosmetic Dentistry-accredited cosmetic dentists in the world. This took five years of case work, presentations, and clinical exams. I was happy to work hard to achieve that designation. The journey was fun and the knowledge critical to practicing top-notch cosmetic dentistry. But as you have probably guessed, I did not celebrate in the big way that most people would after getting this exalted new title. I took a few pictures after the accreditation ceremony and had a nice meal, and then back to work I went. What was next?

In my mind, I felt the achievements were small and not worthy of such attention. There was always someone smarter, faster, or better than me and they should be celebrated, not me.

This pattern of downplaying my accomplishments spread throughout my life like a cancer, infiltrating my career, my hobbies, my relationships, and you name it. I became an overachiever and an under-appreciator, if you will, because I was chasing an idea of perfection. There was something missing in my life, but I could not put my finger on it.

I suppose we need to see one side of the coin to discover the other. It took me a ridiculous amount of time to figure out that perfection does not exist. The pursuit of perfection is okay, but we need to be able to accept that *doing our best* is good enough. I am always just doing my best.

Perfectionism is a dream killer. If you are looking for the *perfect* answer to your questions you will most certainly be disappointed. What is your perfect job? Perfect mate? Perfect purpose? Instead of seeking perfection as commonly defined by humanity, see the perfection in everything around you and accept the fact that you already are perfect. Doing your best is all that you can ask of yourself.

As you gain life experience, your definition of perfection will continue to change, and you will begin to see the beauty in imperfection and how it is responsible for so many beautiful things in our lives.

15 CREATING POSITIVE ENERGY

"If you think you can or can't, you are right."

–Henry Ford

The world is a mirror that reflects our feelings back to us. If we don't like the reflection, then we need to change the feelings that create it. Every thought, statement, and action creates feelings, which are essentially vibrations of energy that we send out to the universe. And like ordering from a menu in a drive-through restaurant, we get what we ask for—even if we are unaware of the fact that we are placing an order and receiving a delivery.

Knowing how the universe works, we really should be more careful. Have you ever heard someone predict bad weather, bad traffic, or some other bad news, and then proudly say "I told you so" when events proved them right? Well, if they only knew that their emotional investment in those negative events was as influential as it really is, perhaps they would aim to be more optimistic. Whenever we attach emotions to a belief, it shapes the outcome of events.

Everything that can happen does, has, and will happen in one universe or another—this is my personal infinite tree of life theory. And our thoughts create our reality. So, let's do our best to create desirable outcomes rather than creating pain and suffering.

Don't like your job? Change it.

Don't like the level of your fitness? Change it.

Don't like the tone of your relationships? Change them.

Let's accept responsibility for the energy underlying our actions, our thoughts, and our emotions, so that we can experience the kind of existence we desire.

The mirror does not judge, it only reflects our state of being. It amplifies our energy and allows us to travel the paths we have selected.

Be careful what you ask for.

Because you are a powerful manifestor, it is critical to make the first hour in the morning count. Immediately when you wake up, you have a choice: positive or negative energy? Which signal do you wish to send out to the mirror for reflection?

Do you complain about the alarm clock going off or it being too early to wake up? Do you start worrying about the day ahead and all the work you anticipate doing? Do you instantly think about your never-ending to-do list?

Or instead, do you wake up and thank the universe for another awesome day and the opportunity to experience life? Do you fill your mind with thoughts of optimism, hope, and gratefulness for all that is? Do you imagine all the things that will go right today, the opportunities you will have, and the adventures and surprises that lie ahead? Do you accept that the challenges that may present themselves to you will be learning experiences and nothing more?

What type of day are you manifesting for yourself? Very different mindsets may begin to shape your day from the moment you wake up.

As silly as it sounds, I now understand why it's good to stand in front of the bathroom mirror smiling and talking to your reflection. Laugh at yourself, smile at yourself, imagine yourself in any positive situation you desire, and thank yourself for the opportunity to achieve it since you are responsible for everything you have in your life. Own the good, the bad, and the ugly. Own your life.

The world reflects all energy we send out. Regardless of whom it is directed at, it always comes back to us. For this reason, we must reserve judgment of others; we really are judging ourselves.

Having a hard time avoiding judgment? Awakening coach Arjuna Ardagh teaches us to add three little words after each judging thought, which results in the removal of all judgment. These three little words are *just like me*. Try it out.

- "That person is impatient, *just like me*."
- "She is so self-centered, *just like me*."
- "He is so arrogant, *just like me*."

Just like me . . . once we begin using these three words it quickly becomes apparent how often we judge and how uncomfortable it feels. If we call someone else arrogant, then we are essentially telling the universe we are arrogant, we like being arrogant, and we would like to become more arrogant. But this is not our highest intention.

Simply changing how you judge other people will have a dramatically positive effect on your life. Judge them in positive terms!

- "She is so beautiful, *just like me*."
- "He is so talented, *just like me*."
- "She has a beautiful smile, *just like me*."

We have all heard the quip "You are what you eat," which is completely true. Taking this one step further, we might also say, "We are what we think."

Aha! Knowing that we have complete control over our body and mind is incredibly freeing, yet it precludes us from blaming others for our current circumstances. We must be willing to take credit for all the good and all the bad.

How do we control the influx of negativity? First and foremost, limit the amount of time you dedicate to watching the news on TV, your iPhone, or the computer. The less news you watch, the better, as news readers put a negative spin on nearly everything. Negative news is entertaining to our animal nature but not so much to our higher nature.

Second, do not immediately jump on social media when you wake up. Put your mobile phone out of reach before you go to bed. Breaking a mobile phone/social media addiction is one of the most difficult things you will ever do, but it's worth it!

Third, avoid negatoids—people who love to spread negativity and flourish around it. You know who they are.

Fourth, meditate. Be aware of the sound of your thoughts but do not listen to them. Quiet your mind.

Controlling the energy you emanate changes what you receive from the world—your mirror. Once you are aware of your sources of negativity, you can shut off those sources and begin filling yourself with positive energy from different sources. In simple terms, you will reap what you sow.

In her book *The Secret,* Rhonda Byrne describes in detail how the law of attraction works. She says that once we establish a positive mindset everything good snowballs in our lives. Of course, negative events will continue to infiltrate our lives, but our positive morning routine and positive intentions will allow us to quickly deny those attacks and move on. Soon we will be a source of positive energy who everyone loves to be around, hoping that some of that magic we have will rub off on them—and it will. Your morning routine is critical to getting the positive energy flowing.

During the day, you also need continuously to add new doses of positive energy into your consciousness to raise the frequency of your energy. How can you do that? Positive attitude and action. Make it routine to smile at everyone and wish them an awesome day, to hold the door for strangers, and to listen to people who talk to you rather than try to jump in and tell them your story. Just thinking positive thoughts works as well.

Here is a short list of things happy, positive people do automatically.

- Smile at everyone
- Hold doors for people
- Wish people an awesome day
- Ask people how they are and listen for an answer

- Think positive thoughts about things all day long, such as: *What a beautiful day, Thank you for this day, I love the blue sky, I love the smell of fresh-cut grass, I love the warm breeze on my face,* and so on
- Immediately forgive negative acts and move on. If somebody cuts us off while driving, immediately let it go. If somebody is nasty to you, smile and walk away
- Clear your mind of negative energy as quickly as you can. Replace a negative thought with a positive thought
- Speak your truth when asked, good or bad. Don't try to please people for fear of a poor reaction. If you do not want to do something when asked, simply say no, thank you.
- If someone wrongs you, calmly tell them how you feel and get over it. Speak your truth, do not sugar coat it, and do not put it off. Most people will respect that and stop looking for trouble with us.
- Respect people. Do not treat them as if they are above or below you. We are all equal at the soul level, so never speak down to someone. Arrogance is one of the worst human traits and is a sign of low self-esteem

- Never say something about someone that you would not tell them directly to his or her face. Gossip is a sign of unhappiness
- Don't take anything personally. You need to be comfortable with who you are, so don't allow the opinions of others to affect you. Be yourself completely. If someone directs a negative statement toward you, let it pass right through you, and forgive them right away. Let it go
- Live in the now. Focus on what is happening at this exact moment, not yesterday or tomorrow. Now is all that matters and all that really exists. Make decisions maximizing the good at this exact moment. If something comes up and you have the option of helping someone or turning a blind eye, help. Don't make excuses, make good actions a reflex.

If you will invest in building a quality consciousness by minding what you say, do, and think, then the world will be your ally.

16 ENJOY THE JOURNEY

*"And then there is the most dangerous risk of all—
the risk of spending your life not doing what you
want on the bet you can buy yourself the freedom to
do it later."*

–Randy Komisar

Everything I have learned about life, both physically
and metaphysically, points toward one important lesson: We must live in the moment. Your perception
of life is unique to you. Mine is unique to me. You
must therefore do your best to enjoy your journey
from birth to death in the way that is most meaning
to your soul. There is no perfect way of living, no one
way that works for everyone the same.

As you begin making positive changes in your life
something strange happens. You start to see the
changes you are making being made everywhere
around you too. When I first began questioning the

sanity of doing something daily that was no longer fulfilling, I did not know what to do about it. Essentially, I was one of those big talkers—all bark, no bite. We all know them. They say: "Someday I will own this joint," "This is only temporary; once I get my ducks in a row, I will travel the world," "I just don't feel this is what I am supposed to be doing," and so forth. Such statements are subtle cries for help.

It took me years until I was so sick and tired of doing the same crap that taking a new action was my only option. You can only listen to so many motivation audios without moving into action before your skin begins to crawl with disgust.

What finally worked? A challenge issued by Ryan Daniel Moran through his Freedom Fast Lane company. It was a simple ten-day challenge designed to make participants think about the future and force them to so something to promote that goal every single day. This challenge was my snowball. After finishing Day 10, I was pumped. I knew I needed to make more changes and now I had a roadmap and was embedded in a community of people who felt the same itch I did.

This was also when the synchronicities that I had been seeing became consistent, letting me know that I was on the right path. My patient pool changed. Now, spiritual, happy people began showing up. Book recommendations from these patients led to more insights, more clarity, more drive to lead a purpose-driven life. The little daily things that had formerly bugged me stopped bugging me so much—like when somebody cut me off while I was driving. Life was slowly but surely becoming easier to endure.

A strange thing happens when you follow your gut: You end up in the right places without even trying. Essentially, what I am saying is that you do not need to know everything before you decide what to do next. The answers will come as you go, so just begin the process. Start your journey of spontaneous living right now. Even though you do not have all the answers yet, you can trust that you will get there. Finding your path and traveling it is where the fun is at anyhow.

17 Pulling It All Together

*"At the center of your being you have the answer;
you know who you are, and you know what you
want."*

–Lao Tzu

I hope that at this point you have a healthy skepticism for what we call reality and some optimism about pursuing your personal path through life. I originally wrote *Unbox Yourself* as a journal for myself, a starting guide, if you will, for me to begin my own unboxing process. And what I have discovered with certainty is that there is no right or wrong way to go about living. That is the truth.

So why not choose a path that makes you happy? You have the power to live a life full of love, laughter, and discovery and to show others that they can do the same.

Let me pull together the gist of what we discussed until now, so you can move ahead with an action plan.

First, you need to decide that you want to unbox yourself. If you are blissfully happy, then more power to you, keep doing whatever you are doing. The rest of us must start by digging into our inner cores to find our passions and our gifts. Asking yourself why you were born can get the ball rolling.

Dig deep, don't leave any stone unturned. Look back at your childhood and what you enjoyed back then: your hobbies, your dreams. Peel back the layers of opinions that got stacked on top of your instincts and inner drive and find out who you really are.

Keep in mind that your purpose is not some difficult riddle, but a simple way to use your gifts and talents to build a better quality of consciousness. Your purpose is to follow your heart as it guides you to action.

We must act because nothing changes if nothing changes. Period. Yet we may find acting in certain ways scary. What are we afraid of anyhow, criticism? Why would you care what anyone thinks of how you wear your hair or the car you drive? How you feel and what you do ideally should be manifested from the inside out. You will have reached a new level of freedom when you are perfectly happy with how perfectly imperfect you are and give yourself permission to be the authentic you everywhere you go. Nobody's opinion about you is worth a solitary dime.

Fear of death? Consciousness does not die, so we do not die; we simply move on to the next game.

Fear of failure? We create failure to learn something. Without it there is no growth. Embrace failure, or as members of the military like to say, embrace the suck. The more you fail, the more you grow. How can you appreciate success if you are not familiar with failure?

If you're in the least bit timid to act, keep in mind that you do not need to take massive action to be successful. Use the snowball technique, where small daily actions grow into massive actions almost effortlessly. Use my guidelines and techniques to hold yourself accountable until your action taking is running on autopilot.

Daily journaling, meditation, and surrounding yourself with likeminded optimistic people is essential. You must have goals: daily goals, short-term goals, and long-term goals. Then decide on the right actions to help you move toward them each day.

Establish daily routines that solidify your path. Most successful souls that I have met have similar daily routines which help them stay on mission. Start with a daily routine like the one I am suggesting and then develop your own.

Next, treat life like the game it is and have fun living it. Seriously, don't sulk over stupid stuff. Don't hold grudges. Go out there and see the positive in everything. Develop an optimistic attitude and learn to laugh at yourself. "This too shall pass" should be everyone's motto, as we all have ups and downs. When you are down get excited because the upswing will most certainly be amazing!

Avoid "negatoids" —people who feed on negative energy that love to spread gossip and bad news.

Find your inner child and let it out—play. Remember these words from George Bernard Shaw: "You don't stop playing because you grow old, you grow old because you stop playing."

There is no rule that says you must be boring and stuffy. Be who you always have been. Don't let the traps of adulthood rob you from your playful nature.

Embrace the message of the movie *Groundhog Day:* Live in the now and make it the best it can be. Yesterday is gone. Tomorrow is not promised. All you have is now. We spend entirely too much time worrying about stuff that most likely will never happen, and even if it does, it won't be that big of a deal.

Once you have unboxed yourself, you will be ready for the next steps of creating a life full of passion! Yes, the fun is only beginning. You will be free to be you, to embrace this amazing thing called life, and I plan to be there right next to you fearlessly exploring

our amazing universe. Go ahead, unbox yourself, find
your why, and join me in living an epic life.

ACKNOWLEDGMENTS

What would life be worth without love and affection from the people around you? Life is about sharing our perfectly imperfect selves with other perfectly imperfect people who make us love, laugh, and sometimes cry. I have had the luxury of being surrounded by some of the most caring, beautiful souls in the world. These souls have carried me when my spirits were low, and they have helped me unbox myself and pointed me toward Samadhi. My mother, my father, and my brother top the long list of such amazing individuals. Thank you.

Most especially, I would like to thank my wife. Behind every strong man stands an even stronger woman. I discovered the truth of this adage from being married to this amazing, intelligent, and beautiful woman for over seventeen years. It means that someone is always there ready to catch you when you fall, which you will, and to help you get back on your feet so you can continue your journey. It means that someone is willingly to postpone her own time in the spotlight, so she can support you. My wife has created a loving home in which I am able to recharge my batteries and my children, she, and I flourish. When everything seems to be going wrong, my wife has the ability to make everything right for us.

I am grateful for the unrelenting love and support I receive from my wife, my family, and my friends. Thank you for believing in me and standing with me, even when my chips are down.

NOTES

Chapter 3: Identifying Your Box

1. Tarthang Tulku. *Skillful Means: Gentle Ways to Successful Work* (Berkeley, CA.: Dharma Publishing, 1978), pp. 5–6.

2. Jim Carrey. Maharishi University of Management Commencement speech May 24, 2014. Available at: https://www.mum.edu/whats-happening/graduation-2014/full-jim-carrey-address-video-and-transcript.

Chapter 4: Why You Were Born

1. *E-Motion*, directed by Frazier Bailey. Passion River, 2015.

2. Steven Kotler. "The Passion Recipe; Four Steps to Total Fulfillment," *Forbes* (March 27, 2015).

Available at: https://www.forbes.com/sites/steven-kotler/2015/03/27/the-passion-recipe-four-steps-to-total-fulfillment/#3c96c49d6bb4.

Chapter 5: Stop Working, Start Playing

1. Marcus Aurelius Antonius. *Meditations,* Book IV: 3 (circa 161–180 C.E.). Available at: https://en.wikiquote.org/wiki/Marcus_Aurelius.

Chapter 11: Act on Your Intentions

1. Les Brown. I jotted this down while watching a video that inspired me and I have forgotten the title.

Chapter 13: Simplify Your Morning Routine

1. Admiral William McRaven. Commencement speech, University of Texas at Austin 2014 graduation ceremony. Available at:
https://news.utexas.edu/2014/05/16/mcraven-urges-graduates-to-find-courage-to-change-the-world.

Resources

Visit my website: www.DrChrisHahn.com

Download your free resources from the book at:
www.DrChrisHahn.com/unboxyourself

Follow my journey on the social networks:
- Instagram: DrChrisHahn
- Facebook: Facebook.com/DrChrisHahn

Hire me as a speaker:
www.DrChrisHahn.com/speaking

Hire me as a coach:
www.DrChrisHahn.com/coaching

Updated Resource List:
www.DrChrisHahn.com/Resources

CHRISTIAN W. HAHN

My Favorite Videos:
Samadhi: Maya, the Illusion of the Self
Inner Worlds Outer Worlds
Sirius
Kalachakra
Arcanum
Cosmic Disclosure
Islands of Inner Peace
The Golden Thread by Joan Halifax
The Healing Effect
The Dalai Lama: Road to Peace
One Track Heart, The Story of Krishna Das
Deepak Chopra: The Happiness Prescription
Super Size Me
Food, Inc.
What the Health
Forks Over Knives
Fat, Sick, and Nearly Dead
The Sugar Film
The Secret by Rhonda Byrne
I AM by Tom Shadyac
What the Bleep Do We Know!?

My Favorite Books and Audios:

The 4-Hour Work Week by Tim Ferriss
Many Lives, Many Masters by Brian L. Weiss
Same Soul, Many Bodies by Brian L. Weiss
Only Love Is Real by Brian L. Weiss
Messages from the Masters by Brian L. Weiss
Journey of Souls: Case Studies by Michael Newton
Destiny of Souls by Michael Newton
Memories of the Afterlife: Life Between Lives
    by Michael Newton
Life Between Lives by Michael Newton
The Untethered Soul by Michael Singer
Your Soul's Plan by Robert Schwartz
Man's Search for Meaning by Viktor E. Frankl
The Book of Joy by Desmond Tutu, Douglas Carlton
    Abrams, and the Dalai Lama
The Power of Now by Eckhart Tolle
A New Earth by Eckhart Tolle
Tao Te Ching by Lao Tzu
Far Journeys by Robert Monroe
Ultimate Journey by Robert Monroe
Start Something That Matters by Blake Mycoskie
The Power of Myth by Joseph Campbell
The Book of Secrets by Deepak Chopra
The School of Greatness by Lewis Howes
Keepers of the Garden by Dolores Cannon
The Travelers Gift by Andy Andrews
The Biology of Belief by Bruce H. Lipton

CHRISTIAN W. HAHN

The Monk Who Sold His Ferrari by Robin Sharma
Spontaneous Evolution: Our Positive Future (and a
   Way to Get There from Here) by Bruce H. Lipton
   and Steve Bhaerman
Conversations with God: An Uncommon Dialogue by
   Neale Donald Walsch

ABOUT THE AUTHOR

Christian W. Hahn, D.D.S., a magna cum laude graduate of University of Southern California Dental School, has practiced as a dentist for over twenty years and is an international speaker for his profession. He lectures on cosmetic dentistry, success, and happiness. Dr. Hahn is one of fewer than 300 AACD-accredited cosmetic dentists in the world and runs a seven-figure dental practice in Louisville, Kentucky, working three days a week. He has invented multiple products, including Frogglez Goggles, which is sold through his company Made By My Dad LLC.

CPSIA information can be obtained
at www.ICGtesting.com
Printed in the USA
FFOW03n1903310518